Houghton Mifflin

Mathematics

Teacher Resource Book

- **Teaching Tools**
- **Family Letters**
- **Just the Facts Worksheets**
  Includes Answer Key and
  Awards Certificates

4

HOUGHTON MIFFLIN

BOSTON • MORRIS PLAINS, NJ

California • Colorado • Georgia • Illinois • New Jersey • Texas

Contents

Teaching Tools

0　$\frac{1}{4}$　$\frac{1}{2}$　1

My Marble Collection

Number of Marbles

28
24
20
16
12
8
0

White Agate　Other Agate　Star Dust　Tiger Eye

Kind of Marble

$$
\begin{array}{r}
25 \\
3{\overline{\smash{\big)}\,75}} \\
-6 \\
\hline
15 \\
-15 \\
\hline
0
\end{array}
$$

Name _____

Dollar Dunk Game Cards

1¢	1¢	1¢	1¢	1¢
1¢	1¢	1¢	1¢	1¢
5¢	5¢	5¢	5¢	5¢
5¢	5¢	5¢	5¢	5¢
10¢	10¢	10¢	10¢	10¢
10¢	10¢	10¢	25¢	25¢
25¢	25¢	25¢	25¢	25¢
25¢	50¢	50¢	50¢	50¢

Name _____

Get the Least Game Board

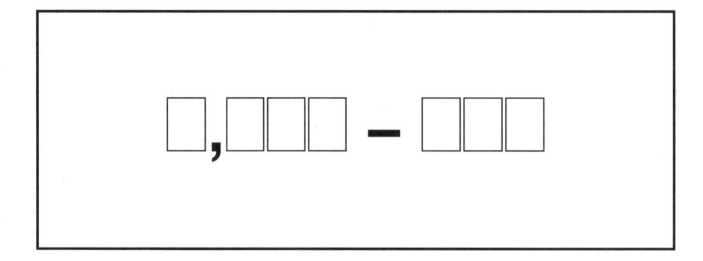

Name _____

Expression Matchup Game Cards

$x + 6$ $x = 3$	9	$m \div 8$ $m = 24$	3
$4 + y$ $y = 2$	6	$2p$ $p = 4$	8
$z - 8$ $z = 10$	2	$5q$ $q = 2$	10
$9 - m$ $m = 4$	5	$d \div 6$ $d = 24$	4

Name _____

Multiplying Does It! Game Cards

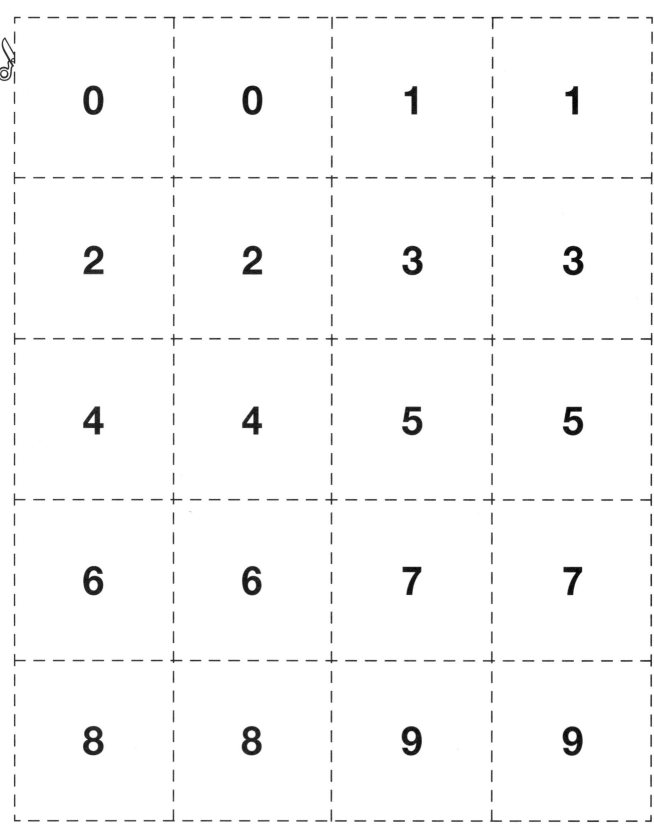

Name _____

Tick-tack-toe Measurement Game Board

the length of your classroom	the width of the chalkboard	the width of your chair
the width of your desk	the height of your chair	the length of a math book
the length of a new pencil	the length of a chalk eraser	the height of your desk

Name _____

Action Fractions Game Cards

1	2	3
4	6	8

Name _____

Tenths Grid

Name _____

Hundredths Grid

Name _____

It All Adds Up Decimal Table

$0.51	$0.62	$0.29	$0.50	$0.48	$0.03
$0.85	$0.22	$0.66	$0.87	$0.19	$0.30
$0.33	$0.70	$0.01	$0.31	$0.94	$0.76
$0.90	$0.04	$0.43	$0.15	$0.25	$0.61

Name _____

It All Adds Up Spinner 1

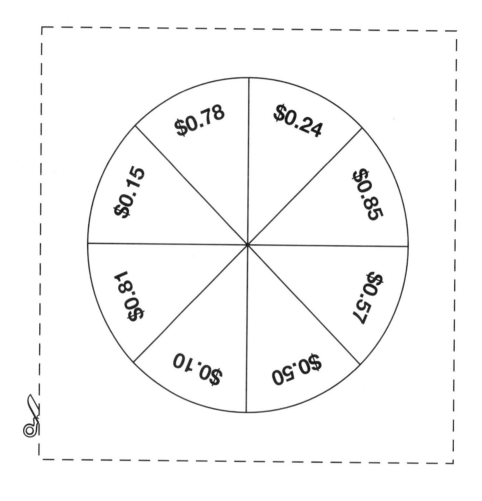

Name _____

It All Adds Up Spinner 2

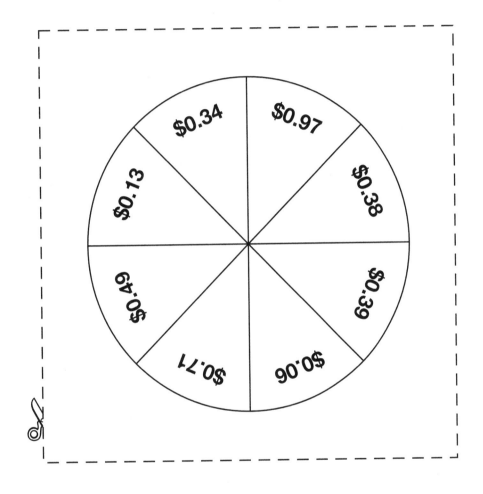

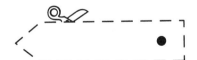

Name _____

Even It Out Paper Squares

Name _____

Even It Out Game Cards

5, 1, 2, 4

2, 8, 5, 1

6, 3, 1, 2

8, 4, 5, 3

6, 5, 2, 3

1, 2, 3, 2

5, 8, 6, 5

Name _____

Making Predictions Probability Cards

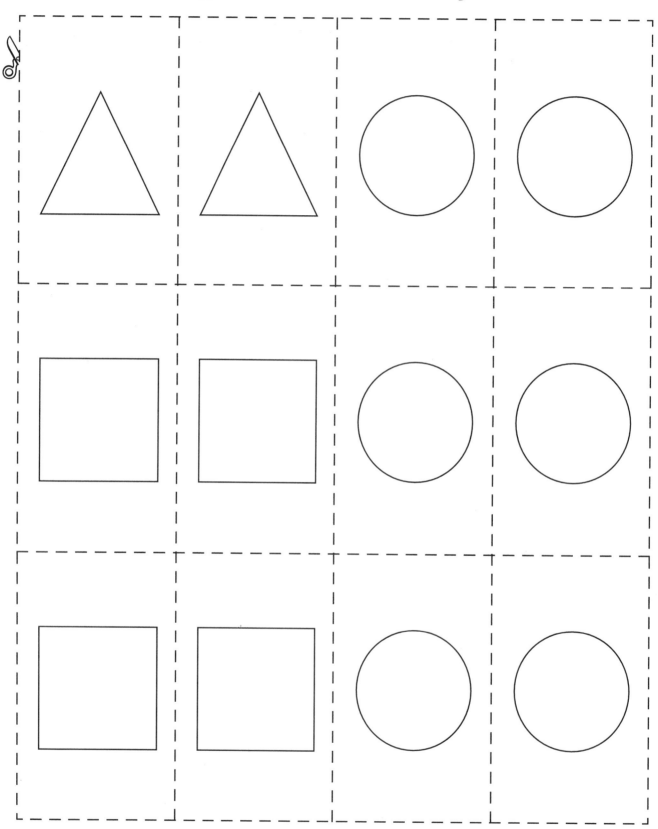

Name _____

Making Predictions **Try It Out**

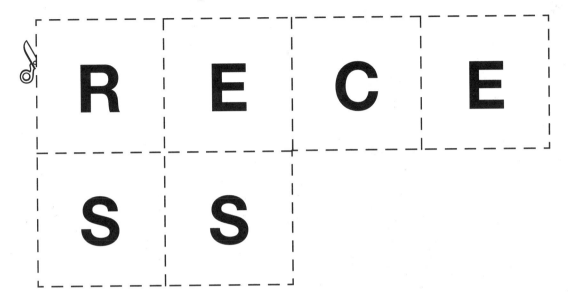

Name _____

Represent Outcomes Tree Diagram

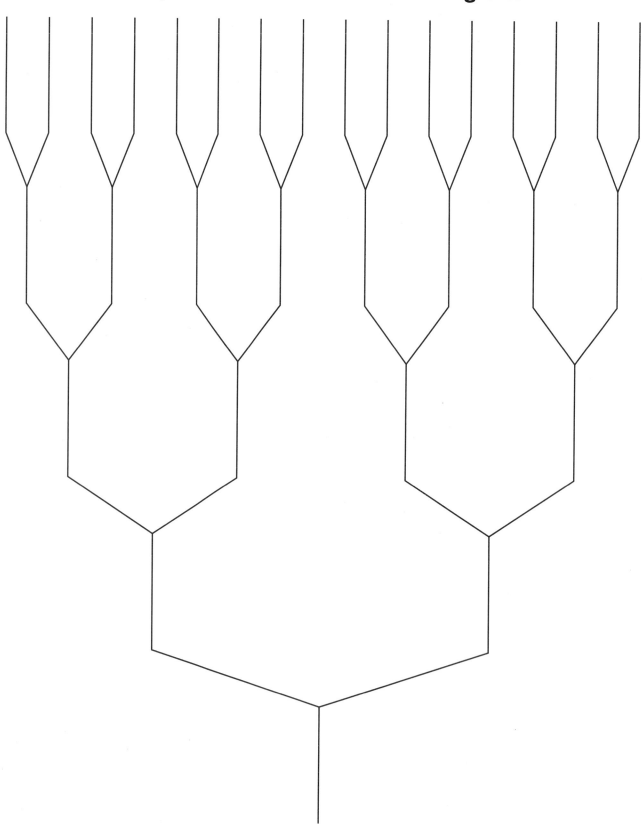

Name _____

Triple Concentration Game Cards

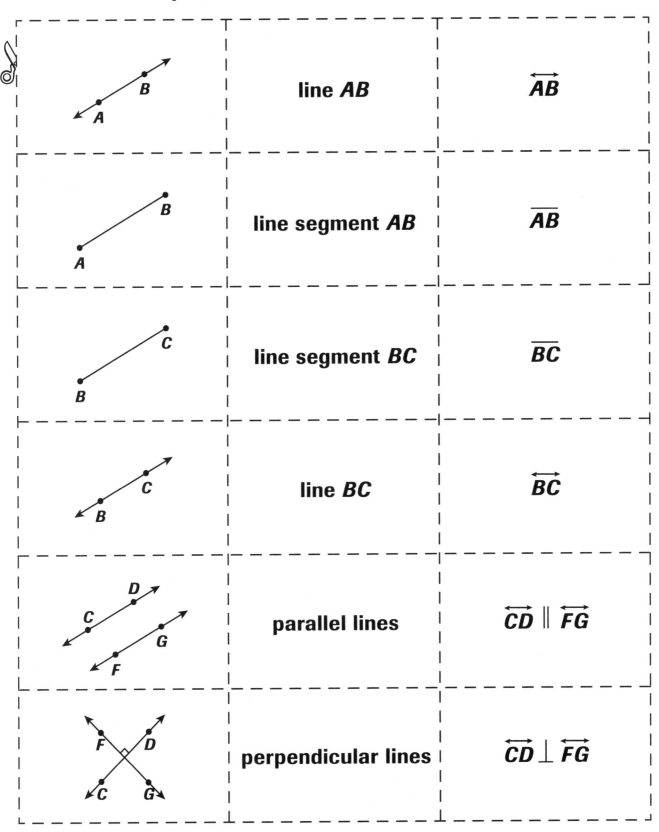

	line **AB**	$\overleftrightarrow{AB}$
	line segment **AB**	$\overline{AB}$
	line segment **BC**	$\overline{BC}$
	line **BC**	$\overleftrightarrow{BC}$
	parallel lines	$\overleftrightarrow{CD} \parallel \overleftrightarrow{FG}$
	perpendicular lines	$\overleftrightarrow{CD} \perp \overleftrightarrow{FG}$

Name _____

Geometry Puzzle Board

Name _____

Geometry Puzzle Pieces

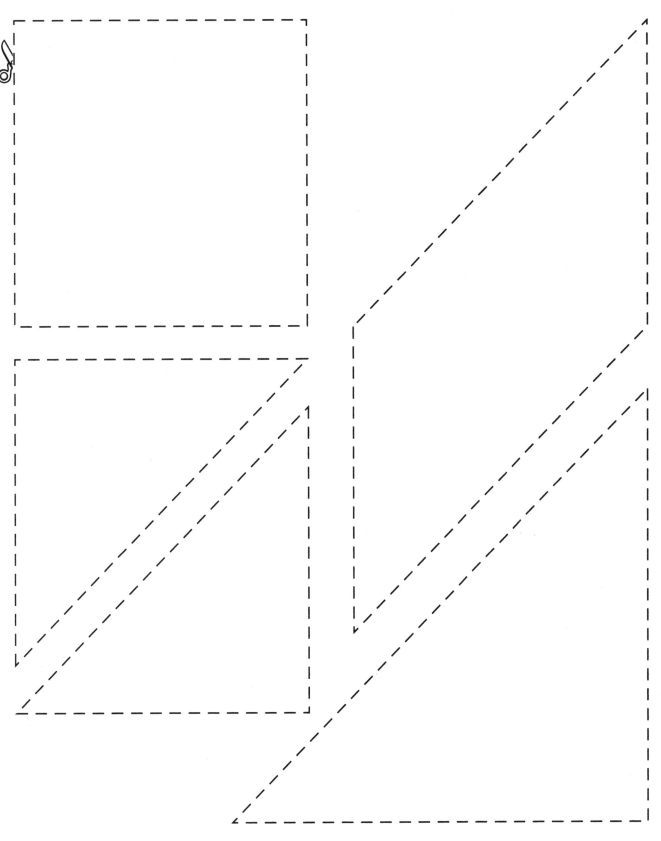

Name _____

Visual Thinking: Making Solid Figures

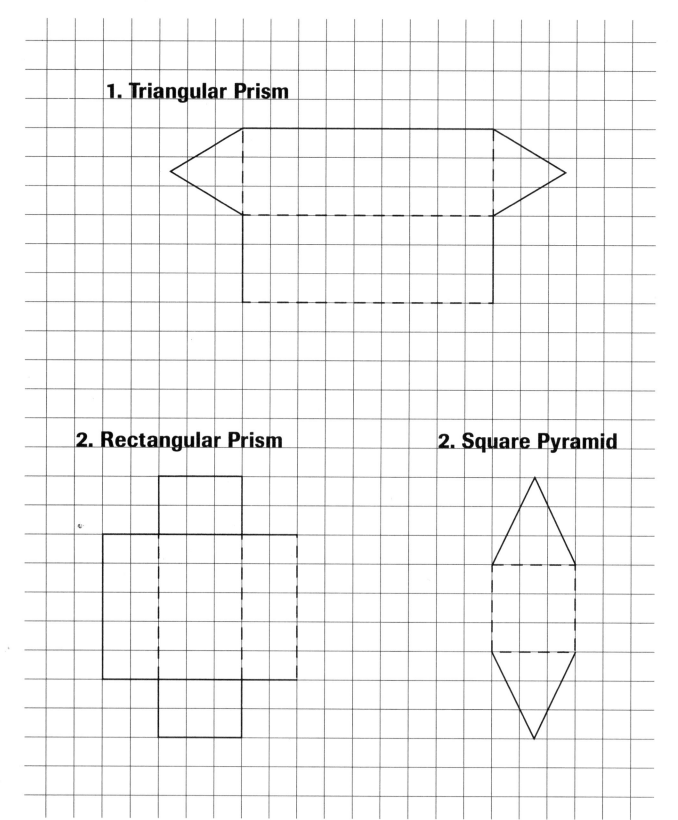

1. Triangular Prism

2. Rectangular Prism

2. Square Pyramid

Name _____

Graph Tick-tack-toe Game Board

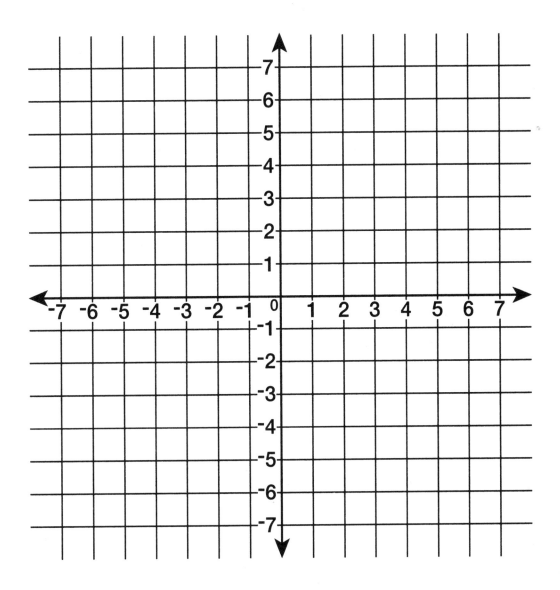

Name _____

Multi-Use Game Cards

Name _____

Answer Sheet 1–50

1. Ⓐ Ⓑ Ⓒ Ⓓ
2. Ⓕ Ⓖ Ⓗ Ⓙ
3. Ⓐ Ⓑ Ⓒ Ⓓ
4. Ⓕ Ⓖ Ⓗ Ⓙ
5. Ⓐ Ⓑ Ⓒ Ⓓ

6. Ⓕ Ⓖ Ⓗ Ⓙ
7. Ⓐ Ⓑ Ⓒ Ⓓ
8. Ⓕ Ⓖ Ⓗ Ⓙ
9. Ⓐ Ⓑ Ⓒ Ⓓ
10. Ⓕ Ⓖ Ⓗ Ⓙ

11. Ⓐ Ⓑ Ⓒ Ⓓ
12. Ⓕ Ⓖ Ⓗ Ⓙ
13. Ⓐ Ⓑ Ⓒ Ⓓ
14. Ⓕ Ⓖ Ⓗ Ⓙ
15. Ⓐ Ⓑ Ⓒ Ⓓ

16. Ⓕ Ⓖ Ⓗ Ⓙ
17. Ⓐ Ⓑ Ⓒ Ⓓ
18. Ⓕ Ⓖ Ⓗ Ⓙ
19. Ⓐ Ⓑ Ⓒ Ⓓ
20. Ⓕ Ⓖ Ⓗ Ⓙ

21. Ⓐ Ⓑ Ⓒ Ⓓ
22. Ⓕ Ⓖ Ⓗ Ⓙ
23. Ⓐ Ⓑ Ⓒ Ⓓ
24. Ⓕ Ⓖ Ⓗ Ⓙ
25. Ⓐ Ⓑ Ⓒ Ⓓ

26. Ⓕ Ⓖ Ⓗ Ⓙ
27. Ⓐ Ⓑ Ⓒ Ⓓ
28. Ⓕ Ⓖ Ⓗ Ⓙ
29. Ⓐ Ⓑ Ⓒ Ⓓ
30. Ⓕ Ⓖ Ⓗ Ⓙ

31. Ⓐ Ⓑ Ⓒ Ⓓ
32. Ⓕ Ⓖ Ⓗ Ⓙ
33. Ⓐ Ⓑ Ⓒ Ⓓ
34. Ⓕ Ⓖ Ⓗ Ⓙ
35. Ⓐ Ⓑ Ⓒ Ⓓ

36. Ⓕ Ⓖ Ⓗ Ⓙ
37. Ⓐ Ⓑ Ⓒ Ⓓ
38. Ⓕ Ⓖ Ⓗ Ⓙ
39. Ⓐ Ⓑ Ⓒ Ⓓ
40. Ⓕ Ⓖ Ⓗ Ⓙ

41. Ⓐ Ⓑ Ⓒ Ⓓ
42. Ⓕ Ⓖ Ⓗ Ⓙ
43. Ⓐ Ⓑ Ⓒ Ⓓ
44. Ⓕ Ⓖ Ⓗ Ⓙ
45. Ⓐ Ⓑ Ⓒ Ⓓ

46. Ⓕ Ⓖ Ⓗ Ⓙ
47. Ⓐ Ⓑ Ⓒ Ⓓ
48. Ⓕ Ⓖ Ⓗ Ⓙ
49. Ⓐ Ⓑ Ⓒ Ⓓ
50. Ⓕ Ⓖ Ⓗ Ⓙ

Name _____

10 x 10 Grid Paper

Name _____

Centimeter Grid

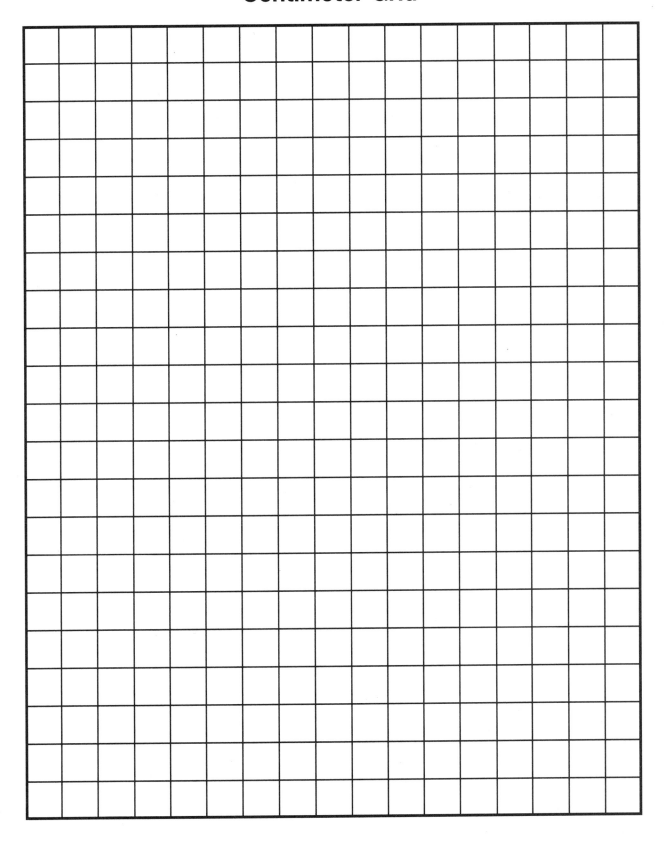

Name _____

Dot Paper

Name _____

Input-Output Tables

Rule:

Input	Output

Rule:

Input	Output

Rule:

Input	Output

Rule:

Input	Output

Rule:

Input	Output

Rule:

Input	Output

Rule:

Input	Output

Rule:

Input	Output

Rule:

Input	Output

Rule:

Input	Output

Rule:

Input	Output

Rule:

Input	Output

Rule:

Input	Output

Rule:

Input	Output

Rule:

Input	Output

Rule:

Input	Output

Rule:

Input	Output

Rule:

Input	Output

Rule:

Input	Output

Rule:

Input	Output

Name _____

Addition Chart

+	0	1	2	3	4	5	6	7	8	9	10
0											
1											
2											
3											
4											
5											
6											
7											
8											
9											
10											

Grade 4, Multi-Use

Name _____

Hundred Chart

1	2	3	4	5	6	7	8	9	10
11	12	13	14	15	16	17	18	19	20
21	22	23	24	25	26	27	28	29	30
31	32	33	34	35	36	37	38	39	40
41	42	43	44	45	46	47	48	49	50
51	52	53	54	55	56	57	58	59	60
61	62	63	64	65	66	67	68	69	70
71	72	73	74	75	76	77	78	79	80
81	82	83	84	85	86	87	88	89	90
91	92	93	94	95	96	97	98	99	100

Name _____

0–99 Chart

0	1	2	3	4	5	6	7	8	9
10	11	12	13	14	15	16	17	18	19
20	21	22	23	24	25	26	27	28	29
30	31	32	33	34	35	36	37	38	39
40	41	42	43	44	45	46	47	48	49
50	51	52	53	54	55	56	57	58	59
60	61	62	63	64	65	66	67	68	69
70	71	72	73	74	75	76	77	78	79
80	81	82	83	84	85	86	87	88	89
90	91	92	93	94	95	96	97	98	99

Name _____

Whole-Number Place-Value Charts

tens	ones

tens	ones

tens	ones

tens	ones

hundreds	tens	ones

hundreds	tens	ones

thousands				ones		
h	t	o	,	h	t	o

thousands				ones		
h	t	o	,	h	t	o

Name _____

Decimal Place-Value Charts

ones		tenths	hundredths
	.		
	.		
	.		
	.		
	.		

ones		tenths	hundredths
	.		
	.		
	.		
	.		
	.		

ones		tenths	hundredths
	.		
	.		
	.		
	.		
	.		

Grade 4, Multi-Use

Name _____

Decimal Models

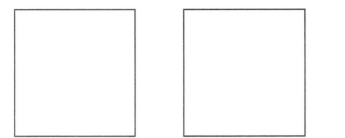

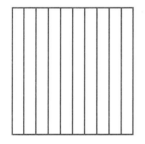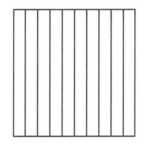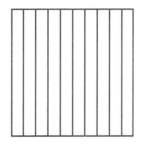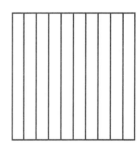

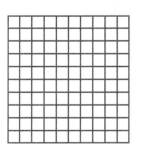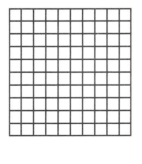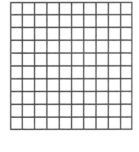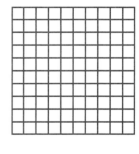

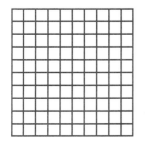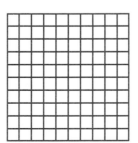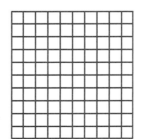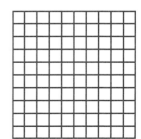

Name _____

Number Lines

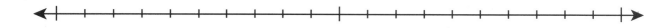

<--|---|---|---|---|---|---|---|---|---|---|---|---|---|---|---|---|---|---|---|---|-->

<--|---|---|---|---|---|---|---|---|---|---|---|---|---|---|---|---|---|---|---|---|-->

<--|---|---|---|---|---|---|---|---|---|---|---|---|---|---|---|---|---|---|---|---|-->

<--|---|---|---|---|---|---|---|---|---|---|-->
10 11 12 13 14 15 16 17 18 19 20

<--|---|---|---|---|---|---|---|---|---|---|-->
0 10 20 30 40 50 60 70 80 90 100

<--|---|---|---|---|---|---|---|---|---|---|-->
0 100 200 300 400 500 600 700 800 900 1,000

<--|---|---|---|---|---|---|---|---|---|---|---|---|---|---|---|---|---|---|---|---|-->
-10 -9 -8 -7 -6 -5 -4 -3 -2 -1 0 +1 +2 +3 +4 +5 +6 +7 +8 +9 +10

<--|---|---|---|---|---|---|---|---|---|---|---|---|---|---|---|---|---|---|---|---|-->
-20 -18 -16 -14 -12 -10 -8 -6 -4 -2 0 +2 +4 +6 +8 +10 +12 +14 +16 +18 +20

Name _____

Blank Clock Faces

Name _____

Fraction Pieces

1

| $\dfrac{1}{2}$ | $\dfrac{1}{2}$ |

| $\dfrac{1}{3}$ | $\dfrac{1}{3}$ | $\dfrac{1}{3}$ |

| $\dfrac{1}{4}$ | $\dfrac{1}{4}$ | $\dfrac{1}{4}$ | $\dfrac{1}{4}$ |

| $\dfrac{1}{5}$ | $\dfrac{1}{5}$ | $\dfrac{1}{5}$ | $\dfrac{1}{5}$ | $\dfrac{1}{5}$ |

| $\dfrac{1}{6}$ | $\dfrac{1}{6}$ | $\dfrac{1}{6}$ | $\dfrac{1}{6}$ | $\dfrac{1}{6}$ | $\dfrac{1}{6}$ |

| $\dfrac{1}{8}$ | $\dfrac{1}{8}$ | $\dfrac{1}{8}$ | $\dfrac{1}{8}$ | $\dfrac{1}{8}$ | $\dfrac{1}{8}$ | $\dfrac{1}{8}$ | $\dfrac{1}{8}$ |

| $\dfrac{1}{10}$ | $\dfrac{1}{10}$ | $\dfrac{1}{10}$ | $\dfrac{1}{10}$ | $\dfrac{1}{10}$ | $\dfrac{1}{10}$ | $\dfrac{1}{10}$ | $\dfrac{1}{10}$ | $\dfrac{1}{10}$ | $\dfrac{1}{10}$ |

| $\dfrac{1}{12}$ | $\dfrac{1}{12}$ | $\dfrac{1}{12}$ | $\dfrac{1}{12}$ | $\dfrac{1}{12}$ | $\dfrac{1}{12}$ | $\dfrac{1}{12}$ | $\dfrac{1}{12}$ | $\dfrac{1}{12}$ | $\dfrac{1}{12}$ | $\dfrac{1}{12}$ | $\dfrac{1}{12}$ |

Name _____

Fraction Circles

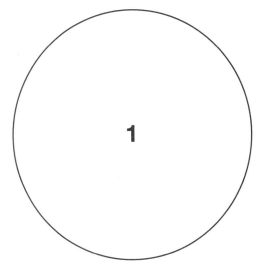 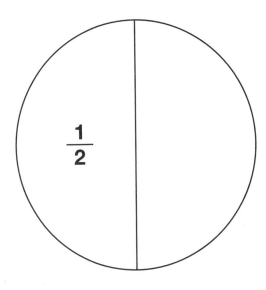

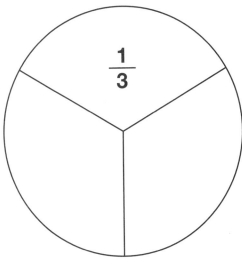 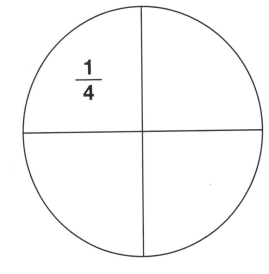

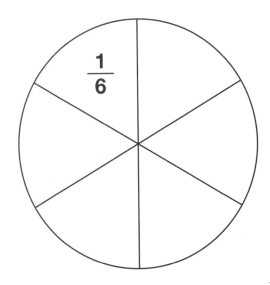 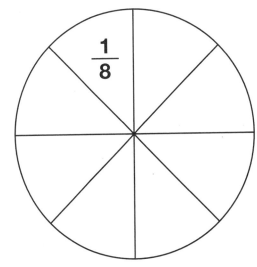

Name _____

Rulers

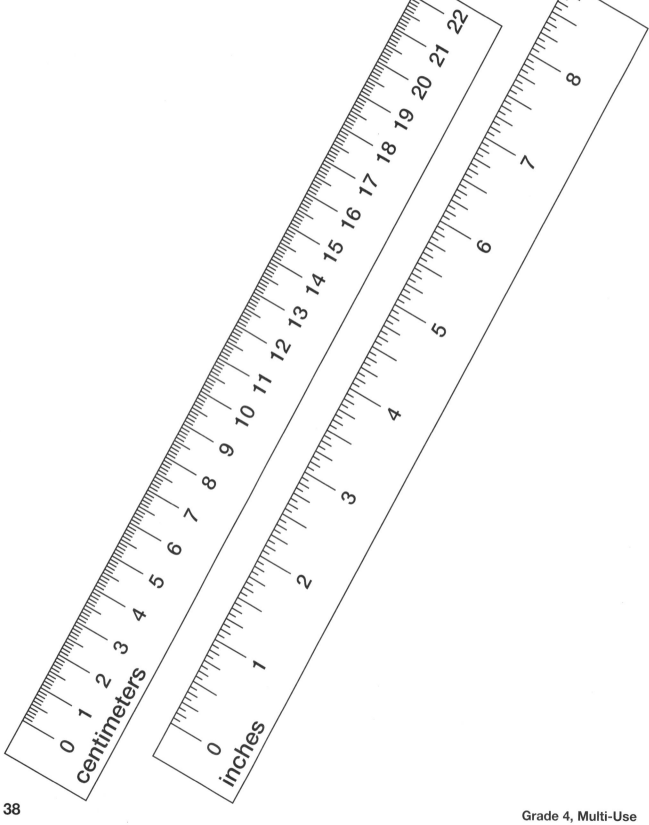

Name _____

Tangram Pieces

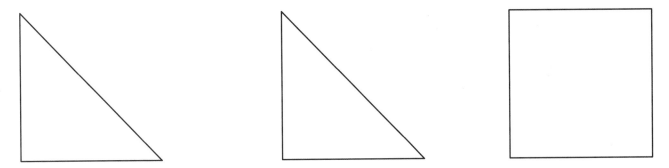

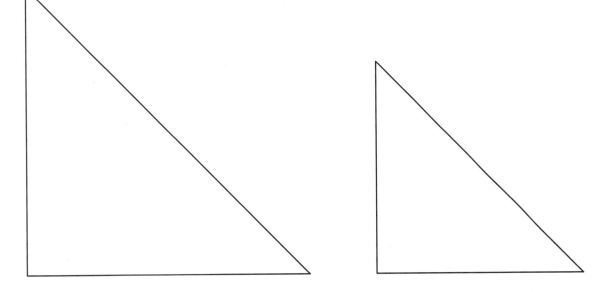

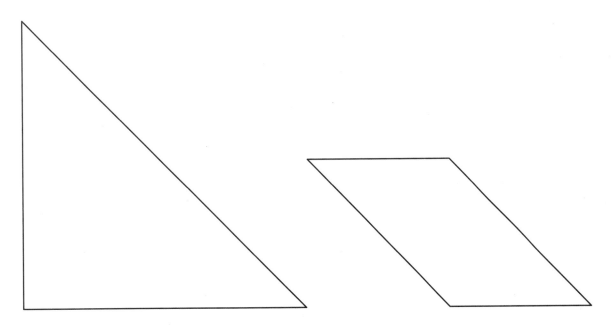

Name _____

Spinners

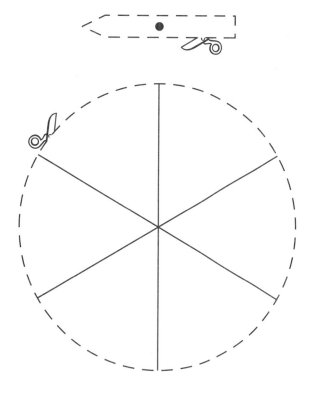

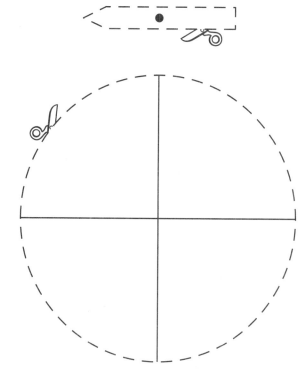

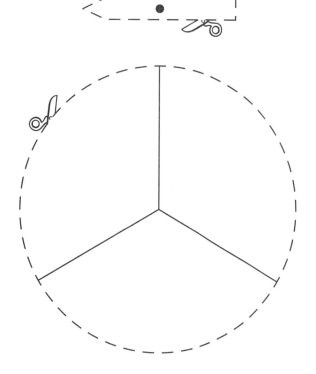

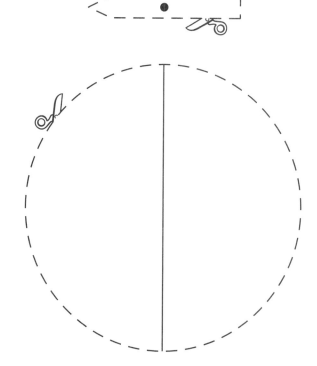

Name _____

First-Quadrant Grids

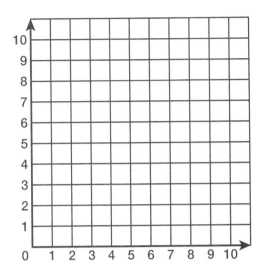
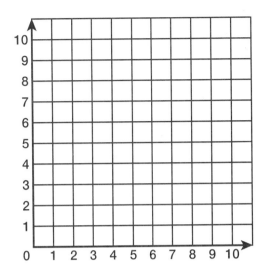
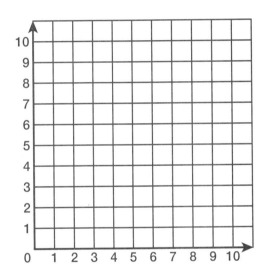
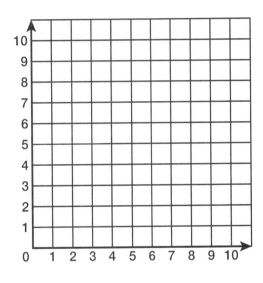
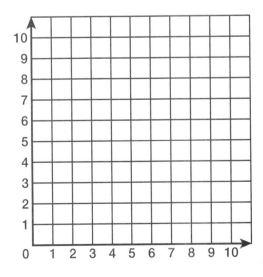
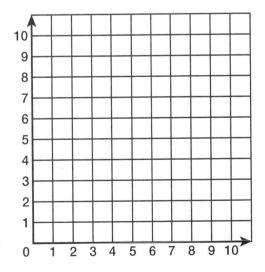

Name _____

Four-Quadrant Grid

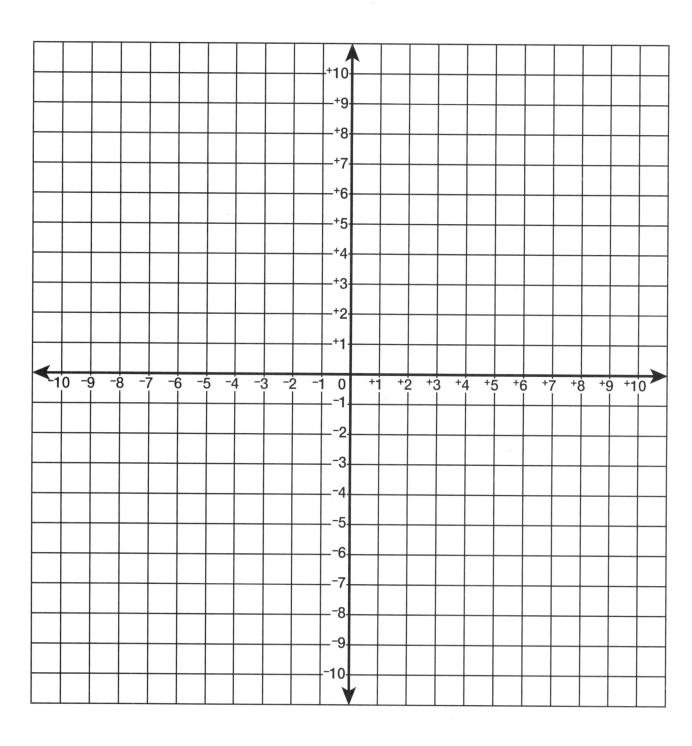

Name _____

Cube Net

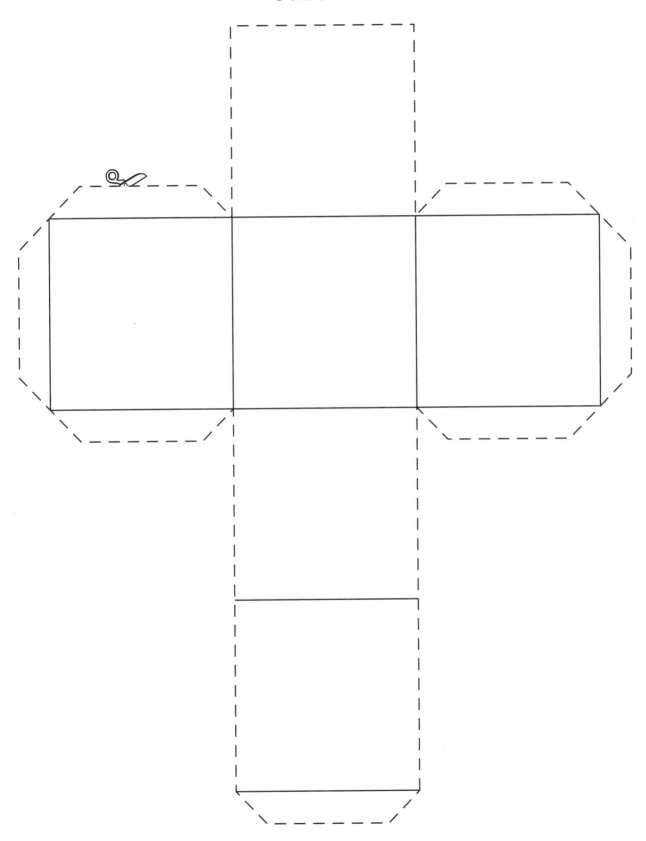

Name _____

Rectangular Prism Net

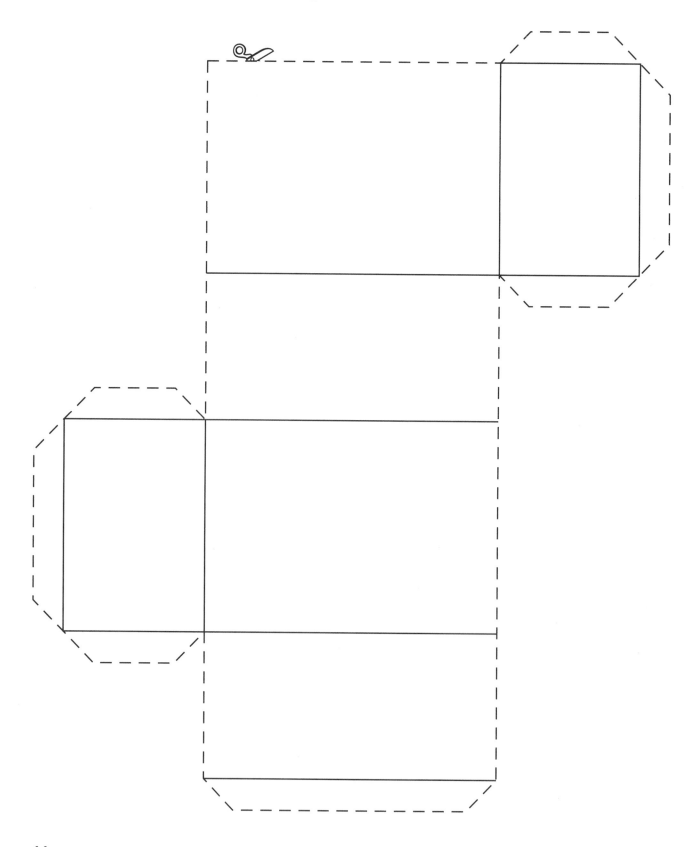

Name _____

Square Pyramid Net

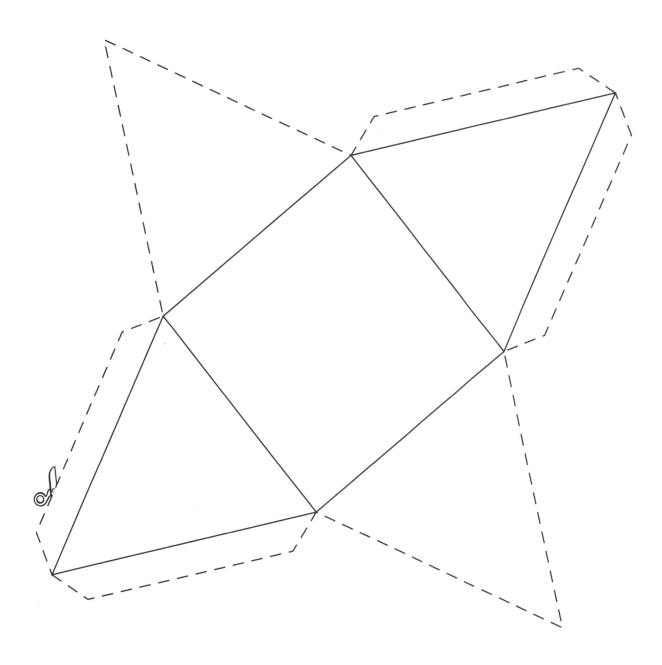

Name _____

Cone Net

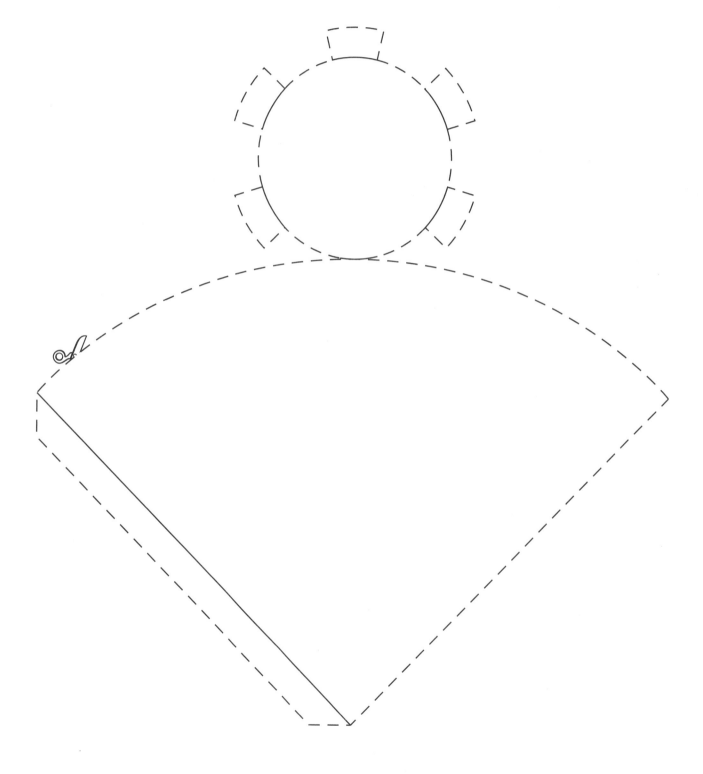

Name _____

Cylinder Net

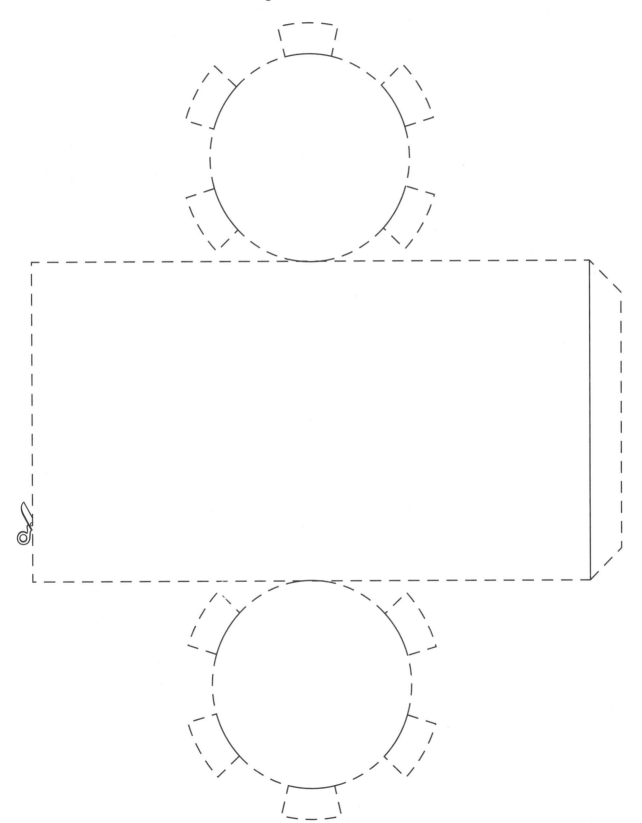

Name _____

Triangular Pyramid Net

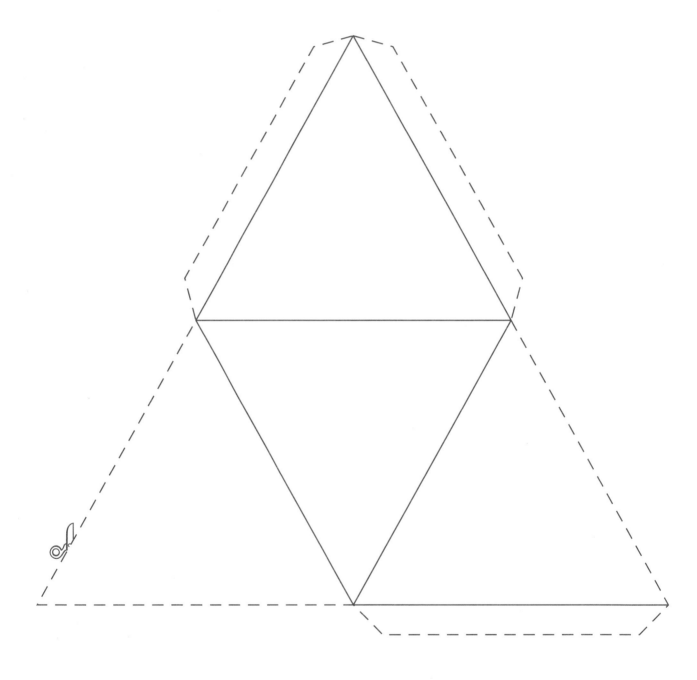

Family
Letters

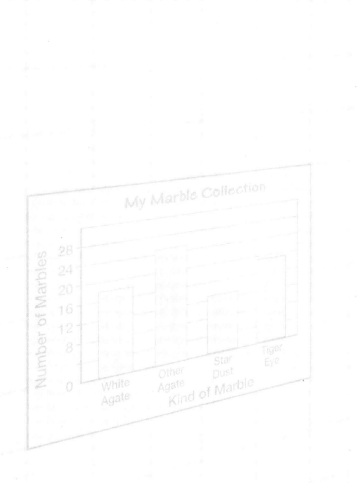

My Marble Collection

Number of Marbles

28
24
20
16
12
8
0

White Agate   Other Agate   Star Dust   Tiger Eye

Kind of Marble

$$\begin{array}{r} 25 \\ 3\overline{)75} \\ -6 \\ \hline 15 \\ -15 \\ \hline 0 \end{array}$$

0    $\frac{1}{4}$ $\frac{1}{2}$ 1

Chapter 1

Family Letter

Dear Family,

During the next few weeks, our math class will be learning about place value of numbers through hundred millions and about money.

You can expect to see work that provides practice with comparing, ordering, and rounding numbers as well as counting and comparing collections of coins.

As we learn how to round numbers, you may wish to use the following sample as a guide.

Vocabulary

estimate A number close to an exact amount. An estimate tells about how much or about how many.

rounding To find about how many or how much by expressing a number to the nearest ten, hundred, thousand, and so on.

Rounding to the Nearest Hundred

To round a number such as 4,175 to the nearest hundred, first find the digit in the rounding place (1).

Next, look at the digit in the place to the right of the rounding place (7).

hundreds place
↓
4,175
↑
greater than 5

- If this digit is less than 5, do not change the digit in the rounding place.
- If it is greater than or equal to 5, increase the digit in the rounding place by 1.
- Then change all of the digits to the right of the rounding place to zeros.

Since the digit to the right of the hundreds place is 7 and 7 is greater than 5, 4,175 rounded to the nearest hundred is 4,200.

Knowing about place value of greater numbers and money will help students solve problems using these kind of numbers.

Sincerely,

Your Child's Teacher

See **www.eduplace.com/parents** for more helpful information.

Family Letter

Dear Family,

Our math class will be spending the next few weeks learning to add and subtract whole numbers. We will also be learning how to use addition and subtraction in expressions and equations.

As we learn how to write and evaluate expressions, you may wish to use the following sample as a guide.

Writing and Evaluating Expressions

Look at the problem to the right. To solve this problem, you can write and then evaluate an expression.

First, write an expression to represent the number of dolls.

- Let b stand for the number of books.
- Then $b + 4$ is the number of dolls.

Then, since you know that there are 6 books, you can evaluate the expression when $b = 6$.

- Write the expression: $b + 4$
- Replace b with 6: $6 + 4$
- Simplify the expression: $6 + 4 = 10$

So, if there are 6 books on the shelf, there are 10 dolls.

During this chapter, students should continue to practice their basic facts for addition and subtraction.

Sincerely,

Your Child's Teacher

Vocabulary

algebraic expression An expression that consists of one or more variables. It could contain some constants and some operations.

evaluating an expression Substituting the values given for the variables and performing the operations to find the value of the expression.

equation A mathematical sentence with an equal sign.

variable A letter or a symbol that represents a number in an algebraic expression.

The number of dolls on a shelf is 4 more than the number of books.

How many dolls are on the shelf if there are 6 books on the shelf?

Safe Site

See **www.eduplace.com/parents** for more helpful information.

Family Letter

Dear Family,

Our math class will be spending the next few weeks learning multiplication and division facts. We will also be learning how to use multiplication and division in expressions and equations.

As you see work that provides practice with the properties of multiplication, you may want to use the following sample as a guide.

Vocabulary

Commutative Property The property which states that the order of the factors does not change the product. It is also called the *Order Property*.

Property of One The product of 1 and any number is that number.

Zero Property If 0 is a factor, the product is 0.

Associative Property The property that states that the order in which factors are grouped does not change the product. It is also called the *Grouping Property*.

Multiplication Properties

Commutative Property	Associative Property
The order in which factors are multiplied does not change the product	The way factors are grouped does not change the product.
$a \times b = b \times a$ $3 \times 6 = 6 \times 3$ $18 = 18$	$(a \times b) \times c = a \times (b \times c)$ $(2 \times 3) \times 4 = 2 \times (3 \times 4)$ $6 \times 4 = 2 \times 12$ $24 = 24$

Zero Property	Property of One
When you multiply any number by 0, the product is 0.	When you multiply any number by 1, the product is that number.
$0 \times a = 0$ $0 \times 5 = 0$	$1 \times a = a$ $1 \times 5 = 5$

During this chapter, students should continue to memorize basic multiplication and division facts.

Sincerely,

Your Child's Teacher

See **www.eduplace.com/parents** for more helpful information.

Family Letter

Dear Family,

During the next few weeks, our math class will be learning about and practicing multiplication of whole numbers.

You can expect to see work that provides practice with multiplying numbers by 1-digit factors as well as by 2-digit factors.

As we learn how to multiply whole numbers and check the exact answer using estimation, you may wish to use this sample as a guide.

Estimating to Check Multiplication

An estimate is a way to check an exact answer. An estimate can be compared to an exact answer to help decide if that answer is reasonable.

First, multiply.

$$\begin{array}{r} {\scriptstyle 2\,2} \\ 267 \\ \times\ 13 \\ \hline 801 \\ 267 \\ \hline 3,471 \end{array}$$

Then, estimate by rounding each factor to the greatest place value.

$$\begin{array}{r} 267 \\ \times\ 13 \\ \hline 3,471 \end{array} \begin{array}{r} \rightarrow\ 300 \\ \rightarrow \times\ 10 \\ \hline 3,000 \end{array}$$

Since 3,000 is close to the exact product, 3,471 is a reasonable answer. If an estimate is not close to the exact answer, the problem should be redone.

During this chapter, students should continue to memorize the basic multiplication facts.

Sincerely,

Your Child's Teacher

Safe Site

See **www.eduplace.com/parents** for more helpful information.

Chapter 5

Family Letter

CHOOLVILLE USA

Dear Family,

During the next few weeks, our math class will be learning about and practicing division of whole numbers.

You can expect to see work that provides practice with dividing numbers with up to four digits by 1-digit numbers.

As we use division to learn about prime and composite numbers, you may wish to use this sample as a guide.

Vocabulary

prime number A whole number that has only itself and 1 as factors.

composite number A whole number that has more than two factors.

divisible One number is divisible by another if the quotient is a whole number and the remainder is 0.

average The number found by dividing the sum of a group of numbers by the number of addends.

Prime and Composite Numbers

You can use the factors of a number to tell if the number is prime or composite. A prime number has only 2 factors, 1 and itself. A composite number has more than 2 factors.

Examples of Prime Numbers		Examples of Composite Numbers	
Prime Number	**Factors**	**Composite Number**	**Factors**
2	1 and 2	6	1, 2, 3, and 6
7	1 and 7	9	1, 3, and 9
11	1 and 11	18	1, 2, 3, 6, 9, and 18
Notice that each number has exactly 2 factors.		Notice that each number has more than two factors.	

2 is the only prime even number. 1 is neither prime nor composite.

During this chapter, students should continue to practice division facts.

Sincerely,

Your Child's Teacher

Safe Site

See **www.eduplace.com/parents** for more helpful information.

Family Letter

Dear Family,

During the next few weeks, our math class will be learning about measurement and negative numbers.

You can expect to see work that provides practice with customary and metric units of measure, perimeter, temperature and negative numbers.

As we learn about negative numbers, you may wish to use this sample as a guide.

Negative Numbers

Temperatures that are below 0° F are negative temperatures. You can think of a thermometer as a vertical number line. The farther down you go, the lower the temperature.

This thermometer shows ⁻10° F. This is read *negative ten degrees Fahrenheit* or *ten degrees below zero.*

You can use a thermometer to find the difference between a positive and a negative temperature. This thermometer shows how to find the difference between ⁻10° F and 7° F.

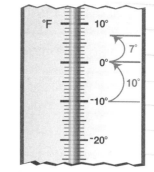

10 + 7 = 17
The difference is 17°.

Knowing about measurement and negative numbers will help students solve problems using these concepts in everyday life.

Sincerely,

Your Child's Teacher

See **www.eduplace.com/parents** for more helpful information.

Family Letter

Dear Family,

During the next few weeks, our math class will be learning about fractions, mixed numbers, and adding and subtracting mixed numbers with like denominators.

When you see work that provides practice writing equivalent fractions, you may wish to use this sample as a guide.

Vocabulary

equivalent fractions Fractions that show different numbers with the same value.

simplest form A fraction whose numerator and denominator have the number 1 as the only factor.

improper fraction A fraction that is greater than or equal to 1. The numerator in an improper fraction is greater than or equal to the denominator.

Writing Equivalent Fractions

You can use multiplication or division to write equivalent fractions.

- To write equivalent fractions for $\frac{4}{5}$, you can multiply the denominator and the numerator by the same number. For example:

$$\frac{4 \times 2}{5 \times 2} = \frac{8}{10} \qquad \frac{4 \times 4}{5 \times 4} = \frac{16}{20} \qquad \frac{4 \times 10}{5 \times 10} = \frac{40}{50}$$

The fractions $\frac{8}{10}$, $\frac{16}{20}$, and $\frac{40}{50}$ are equivalent to $\frac{4}{5}$.

- To write equivalent fractions for $\frac{32}{48}$, you can divide the denominator and the numerator by the same number. For example:

$$\frac{32 \div 2}{48 \div 2} = \frac{16}{24} \qquad \frac{32 \div 8}{48 \div 8} = \frac{4}{6} \qquad \frac{32 \div 16}{48 \div 16} = \frac{2}{3}$$

The fractions $\frac{16}{24}$, $\frac{4}{6}$, and $\frac{2}{3}$ are equivalent to $\frac{32}{48}$.

Knowing about fractions will help students solve problems that include fractional numbers.

Sincerely,

Your Child's Teacher

See **www.eduplace.com/parents** for more helpful information.

Family Letter

Dear Family,

During the next few weeks, our math class will be learning about decimals.

You can expect to see work that provides practice with relating fractions, mixed numbers, and decimals; comparing and ordering decimals; and adding and subtracting decimals.

As we learn how to compare and order decimals, you may wish to use this sample as a guide.

Comparing and Ordering Decimals

To arrange these decimals in order from greatest to least, follow these steps.

2.04   1.9   3.1   2.77

- Place the numbers in a place-value chart.
- Compare the digits in the greatest place first.

  3 is the greatest digit, so 3.1 is the greatest number.

  1 is the least digit, so 1.9 is the least number.

ones		tenths	hundredths
2	.	0	4
1	.	9	0
3	.	1	0
2	.	7	7

- There are two numbers that have a 2 in the ones place. To compare these numbers, compare the digits in the tenths place.

  7 > 0, so 2.77 > 2.04.

The numbers in order from greatest to least are

3.1   2.77   2.04   1.9

Knowing about decimals will help students solve problems that include decimal numbers.

Sincerely,

Your Child's Teacher

See **www.eduplace.com/parents** for more helpful information.

Family Letter

Dear Family,

During the next few weeks, our math class will be learning about statistics and probability.

You can expect to see work that provides practice with graphing, finding mode, median, mean, and range, and using probability concepts.

As we learn how to find the median, you may wish to use this sample as a guide.

Vocabulary

median The middle number when a set of numbers is arranged in order from least to greatest.

double bar graph A graph in which information is shown by means of pairs of rectangular bars drawn next to each other.

line graph A graph that uses a broken line to show changes in data.

tree diagram A diagram that shows combinations of outcomes of an event.

Finding the Median

The median is the middle number in a set of data when that data is arranged in order from least to greatest. Look at these examples:

Find the median when there is an odd number of numbers in the data set.	Find the median when there is an even number of numbers in the data set.
12 13 13 **13** 15 15 16	12 13 13 **13** **15** 15 16 16
13 is the middle number, so 13 is the median.	When there are two middle numbers, add the numbers and divide the sum by 2.
	$13 + 15 = 28$ $28 \div 2 = 14$
	The median is 14.

Understanding data and how it is displayed will help students evaluate information they encounter in the real world.

Sincerely,

Your Child's Teacher

Safe Site

See **www.eduplace.com/parents** for more helpful information.

Family Letter

Dear Family,

During the next few weeks, our math class will be identifying plane and solid figures as well as finding perimeter, area, and volume.

As we learn how to find the perimeter and area of a rectangle using formulas, you may wish to use this sample as a guide.

Vocabulary

radius A segment that connects the center of a circle to any point on a circle.

diameter A segment that connects two points on the circle and passes though the center.

scalene triangle A triangle with all sides of different lengths.

acute triangle A triangle in which each of the three angles is acute.

obtuse triangle A triangle that has one obtuse angle.

Finding Perimeter and Area

To find the perimeter and area of this rectangle, follow these steps.

6 ft

10 ft

- Perimeter is the sum of the lengths of the sides of a figure. To find the perimeter of a rectangle, you can use either of these formulas:

$P = l + w + l + w$
$P = 10 \text{ ft} + 6 \text{ ft} + 10 \text{ ft} + 6 \text{ ft}$
$P = 32 \text{ ft}$

$P = (2 \times l) + (2 \times w)$
$P = (2 \times 10 \text{ ft}) + (2 \times 6 \text{ ft})$
$P = 20 \text{ ft} + 12 \text{ ft}$
$P = 32 \text{ ft}$

The perimeter of the rectangle is 32 ft

- Area is the number of square units inside a figure. To find the area of a rectangle, you can use this formula.

$A = l \times w$
$A = 10 \text{ ft} \times 6 \text{ ft}$
$A = 60 \text{ ft}^2$

The area of the rectangle is 60 ft².

Knowing about geometric figures will help students understand the geometry that is all around them.

Sincerely,

Your Child's Teacher

Safe Site

See **www.eduplace.com/parents** for more helpful information.

Family Letter

Dear Family,

During the next few weeks, our math class will be learning about graphing and algebra.

You can expect to see work that provides practice with plotting and locating points on a coordinate graph, as well as working with integers.

As we learn how to graph ordered pairs on a coordinate graph, you may wish to use this sample as a guide.

Vocabulary

coordinates An ordered pair of numbers that locates a point in the coordinate plane.

integers Positive and negative whole numbers and 0.

x-coordinate The first number of an ordered pair of numbers that corresponds to a point in a coordinate system.

y-coordinate The second number of an ordered pair of numbers that corresponds to a point in a coordinate system.

Graphing Ordered Pairs

When graphing an ordered pair, the x-coordinate is first, and it tells you to move right or left. The y-coordinate is second, and it tells you to move up or down.

(5, 3)	(⁻3, 2)	(4, ⁻5)	(⁻2, ⁻4)

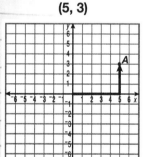 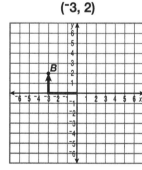 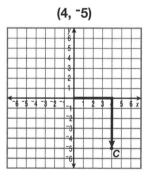 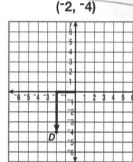

Knowing about graphing and algebra will lay the foundation for the math that students will learn in the years to come.

Sincerely,

Your Child's Teacher

Safe Site

See **www.eduplace.com/parents** for more helpful information.

Family Letter

Dear Family,

During the next few weeks, our math class will be learning about division of whole numbers by 2-digit numbers.

You can expect to see work that provides practice with estimating quotients and dividing by a 2-digit number. You may wish to use this sample as a guide.

2-Digit Quotients

To find $2,180 \div 29$, you can follow these steps.

Step 1: Estimate to decide what the first digit of the quotient should be and where in the quotient it should go.	**Step 2:** Try the estimate. If it works, divide. If not, adjust your estimate and try again.
$$29\overline{)2,180} \rightarrow \overset{70}{30\overline{)2,100}}$$	$$\begin{array}{r}7 \\ 29\overline{)2,180} \\ -2\,03 \\ \hline 15\end{array}$$ Think: $\overset{7 \text{ tens}}{30\overline{)210 \text{ tens}}}$ Multiply. 7×29 Subtract. $218 - 203$ Compare. $15 < 29$
Step 3: Bring down the ones. Estimate, then divide.	**Step 4:** Check the answer by multiplying.
$$\begin{array}{r}75 \text{ R}5 \\ 29\overline{)2,180} \\ -2\,03\downarrow \\ \hline 150 \\ -145 \\ \hline 5\end{array}$$ Think: $5 \atop 30\overline{)150}$ Multiply. 5×29 Subtract. $150 - 145$ Compare. $5 < 29$	$$\begin{array}{r}75 \\ \times\ 29 \\ \hline 675 \\ 150 \\ \hline 2,175 \\ +\quad 5 \\ \hline 2,180\end{array}$$ The sum equals the dividend, so the quotient is correct.

Knowing how to divide with greater numbers will help students solve problems that involve division.

Sincerely,

Your Child's Teacher

See **www.eduplace.com/parents** for more helpful information.

Just the Facts Worksheets

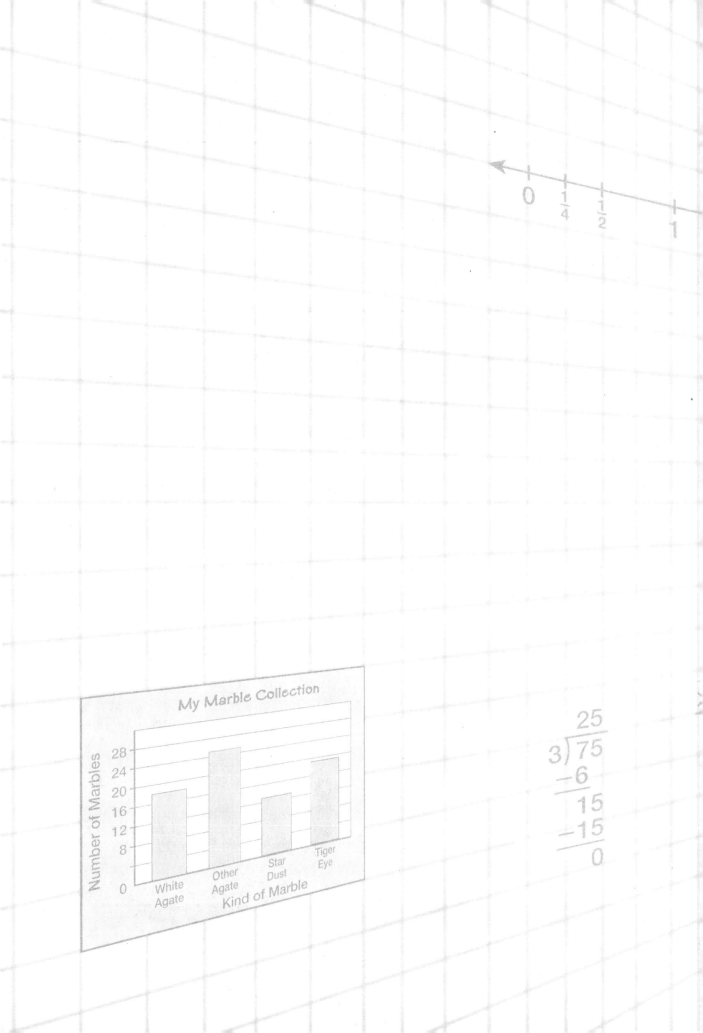

0   $\frac{1}{4}$ $\frac{1}{2}$ 1

My Marble Collection

Number of Marbles

28
24
20
16
12
8
0

White Agate   Other Agate   Star Dust   Tiger Eye

Kind of Marble

$$\begin{array}{r} 25 \\ 3\overline{)75} \\ -6 \\ \hline 15 \\ -15 \\ \hline 0 \end{array}$$

Name_____ Date _____

 # BASIC FACTS

Addition and Subtraction Facts

Add.

1.   2
  + 4
	2. 3
	  + 5
		3. 8
		  + 1
			4. 3
			  + 4
				5. 7
				  + 2

6.   1
  + 0
	7. 2
	  + 6
		8. 2
		  + 8
			9. 7
			  + 1
				10. 0
				  + 6

Add or subtract. Find a pattern. Write the next number sentence.

11. 1 + 6 = _____

2 + 6 = _____

3 + 6 = _____

_____ + _____ = _____

12. 3 + 3 = _____

4 + 3 = _____

5 + 3 = _____

_____ + _____ = _____

13. 7 − 2 = _____

8 − 2 = _____

9 − 2 = _____

_____ − _____ = _____

14. 9 − 5 = _____

9 − 6 = _____

9 − 7 = _____

_____ − _____ = _____

Name_____ Date _____

BASIC FACTS

Addition and Subtraction Facts

Find the greater number. Count on to add.

1. 6 + 1 = _____   **2.** 3 + 4 = _____   **3.** 5 + 2 = _____

4. 3 + 7 = _____   **5.** 6 + 2 = _____   **6.** 1 + 8 = _____

7. 2 + 9 = _____   **8.** 3 + 5 = _____   **9.** 4 + 2 = _____

Find the difference.

10. 5 − 3	**11.** 7 − 4	**12.** 8 − 6	**13.** 10 − 7	**14.** 4 − 0
15. 6 − 5	**16.** 4 − 2	**17.** 9 − 6	**18.** 6 − 4	**19.** 7 − 6
20. 5 − 2	**21.** 6 − 3	**22.** 8 − 5	**23.** 7 − 3	**24.** 6 − 0
25. 9 − 3	**26.** 8 − 2	**27.** 9 − 5	**28.** 4 − 3	**29.** 7 − 5

Name_____ Date _____

BASIC FACTS

Doubles, Near Doubles Addition and Subtraction Facts

Write a double that helps. Add.

1. 6 + 5 + _____	**2.** 8 + 9 + _____	**3.** 7 + 6 + _____
4. 6 + 5 + _____	**5.** 8 + 9 + _____	**6.** 7 + 8 + _____

Find the difference.

7. 5 − 3	**8.** 7 − 4	**9.** 8 − 6	**10.** 10 − 5	**11.** 4 − 0
12. 16 − 8	**13.** 4 − 2	**14.** 12 − 6	**15.** 8 − 4	**16.** 7 − 6

Look for doubles first. Then add.

17. $2 + 2 + 4 =$ _____   **18.** $3 + 3 + 5 =$ _____

19. $4 + 5 + 5 =$ _____   **20.** $7 + 7 + 3 =$ _____

Name_____   Date _____

BASIC FACTS

Doubles, Near Doubles Addition and Subtraction Facts

Add.

1.	4 + 4	2.	7 + 6	3.	2 + 8	4.	6 + 3	5.	4 + 5

6.	9 + 9	7.	5 + 5	8.	3 + 3	9.	5 + 6	10.	8 + 7

11.	8 + 8	12.	1 + 2	13.	6 + 6	14.	7 + 7	15.	3 + 7

Draw a line to match. Subtract.

16. $16 - 8 =$ _____   **A.** 18
− 9

17. $9 - 5 =$ _____   **B.** 16
− 8

18. $18 - 9 =$ _____   **C.** 9
− 5

Name_____ Date _____

 # BASIC FACTS

Using Ten to Add and Subtract

Add. Make a ten to help.

1. $9 + 5 =$ _____   **2.** $4 + 7 =$ _____   **3.** $5 + 8 =$ _____

4. $6 + 8 =$ _____   **5.** $4 + 9 =$ _____   **6.** $7 + 9 =$ _____

7. $8 + 9 =$ _____   **8.** $4 + 8 =$ _____   **9.** $9 + 6 =$ _____

Subtract.

10. $\begin{array}{r} 10 \\ -\ 3 \\ \hline \end{array}$
11. $\begin{array}{r} 6 \\ -\ 4 \\ \hline \end{array}$
12. $\begin{array}{r} 7 \\ -\ 5 \\ \hline \end{array}$
13. $\begin{array}{r} 9 \\ -\ 6 \\ \hline \end{array}$
14. $\begin{array}{r} 8 \\ -\ 3 \\ \hline \end{array}$

15. $\begin{array}{r} 6 \\ -\ 2 \\ \hline \end{array}$
16. $\begin{array}{r} 10 \\ -\ 2 \\ \hline \end{array}$
17. $\begin{array}{r} 11 \\ -\ 1 \\ \hline \end{array}$
18. $\begin{array}{r} 10 \\ -\ 8 \\ \hline \end{array}$
19. $\begin{array}{r} 11 \\ -\ 9 \\ \hline \end{array}$

20. $\begin{array}{r} 8 \\ -\ 5 \\ \hline \end{array}$
21. $\begin{array}{r} 7 \\ -\ 4 \\ \hline \end{array}$
22. $\begin{array}{r} 7 \\ -\ 6 \\ \hline \end{array}$
23. $\begin{array}{r} 8 \\ -\ 2 \\ \hline \end{array}$
24. $\begin{array}{r} 9 \\ -\ 7 \\ \hline \end{array}$

25. $\begin{array}{r} 11 \\ -\ 3 \\ \hline \end{array}$
26. $\begin{array}{r} 10 \\ -\ 7 \\ \hline \end{array}$
27. $\begin{array}{r} 8 \\ -\ 6 \\ \hline \end{array}$
28. $\begin{array}{r} 10 \\ -\ 4 \\ \hline \end{array}$
29. $\begin{array}{r} 8 \\ -\ 4 \\ \hline \end{array}$

Name_____ Date _____

BASIC FACTS

Using Ten to Add and Subtract

Subtract. Make a ten to help.

1. $13 - 8 =$ _____

2. $15 - 9 =$ _____

3. $16 - 8 =$ _____

4. $12 - 9 =$ _____

5. $14 - 8 =$ _____

6. $17 - 8 =$ _____

Add or subtract.

7. $9 + 6 =$ _____

8. $16 - 8 =$ _____

9. $4 + 9 =$ _____

10. $18 - 9 =$ _____

11. $13 - 5 =$ _____

12. $7 + 7 =$ _____

13. $11 - 6 =$ _____

14. $14 - 8 =$ _____

15. $7 + 8 =$ _____

16. $12 - 7 =$ _____

17. $6 + 6 =$ _____

18. $10 - 6 =$ _____

19. $17 - 9 =$ _____

20. $9 + 7 =$ _____

21. $13 - 8 =$ _____

22. $15 - 8 =$ _____

23. $5 + 6 =$ _____

24. $7 + 9 =$ _____

Find the missing number.

25. $12 -$ _____ $= 3$

26. $14 -$ _____ $= 7$

27. $11 -$ _____ $= 9$

28. $16 -$ _____ $= 7$

29. $13 -$ _____ $= 5$

30. $12 -$ _____ $= 7$

Name_____ Date _____

BASIC FACTS

Naming and Using Arrays in Multiplication

Write one addition sentence and one multiplication sentence to describe each array.

1. • • • • •
   • • • • •
   • • • • •

   _____ = _____

   _____ = _____

2. • • • • • • •
   • • • • • • •

   _____ = _____

   _____ = _____

Solve.

3. 2 + 2 = _____

   2 × 2 = _____

4. 2 + 2 + 2 = _____

   3 × 2 = _____

5. 2 + 2 + 2 + 2 = _____

   4 × 2 = _____

6. 2 + 2 + 2 + 2 + 2 = _____

   5 × 2 = _____

7. 9 × 2 = _____

8. 8 × 2 = _____

Draw counters to show the array. Then write the product.

9.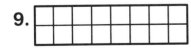

   2 × 7 = _____

10. 6 × 2 = _____

11. 4 × 2 = _____

Name_____   Date _____

BASIC FACTS

Naming and Using Arrays in Multiplication

Draw counters to show the array. Then find the product.

1.

$3 \times 6 =$ _____

2.

$3 \times 8 =$ _____

3.

$3 \times 5 =$ _____

Multiply. Think of doubles or the order property.

4. $2 \times 7 =$ _____   **5.** $6 \times 2 =$ _____   **6.** $2 \times 9 =$ _____

7. $4 \times 2 =$ _____   **8.** $2 \times 8 =$ _____   **9.** $2 \times 5 =$ _____

10. $2 \times 3 =$ _____   **11.** $9 \times 2 =$ _____   **12.** $2 \times 2 =$ _____

13. $5 \times 3 =$ _____   **14.** $4 \times 3 =$ _____   **15.** $3 \times 7 =$ _____

Use estimation. Write < or >.

16. $4 \times 3 = 12$, so 3×3 _____ 12   **17.** $7 \times 2 = 14$, so 7×3 _____ 14

18. $3 \times 2 = 6$, so 4×2 _____ 6   **19.** $8 \times 3 = 24$, so 9×3 _____ 24

20. $3 \times 3 = 9$, so 4×3 _____ 9   **21.** $6 \times 3 = 18$, so 7×3 _____ 18

Name_____ Date _____

BASIC FACTS

Multiplying by 1 and 2

Multiply.

1.   1
   ×2
	2. 2
	   ×3
		3. 4
		   ×1
			4. 1
			   ×7
				5. 6
				   ×2

1. $\begin{array}{r}1\\ \times 2\\ \hline\end{array}$ 2. $\begin{array}{r}2\\ \times 3\\ \hline\end{array}$ 3. $\begin{array}{r}4\\ \times 1\\ \hline\end{array}$ 4. $\begin{array}{r}1\\ \times 7\\ \hline\end{array}$ 5. $\begin{array}{r}6\\ \times 2\\ \hline\end{array}$

6. $\begin{array}{r}1\\ \times 1\\ \hline\end{array}$ 7. $\begin{array}{r}7\\ \times 1\\ \hline\end{array}$ 8. $\begin{array}{r}9\\ \times 2\\ \hline\end{array}$ 9. $\begin{array}{r}1\\ \times 8\\ \hline\end{array}$ 10. $\begin{array}{r}1\\ \times 5\\ \hline\end{array}$

11. $\begin{array}{r}4\\ \times 2\\ \hline\end{array}$ 12. $\begin{array}{r}1\\ \times 6\\ \hline\end{array}$ 13. $\begin{array}{r}2\\ \times 2\\ \hline\end{array}$ 14. $\begin{array}{r}1\\ \times 4\\ \hline\end{array}$ 15. $\begin{array}{r}1\\ \times 3\\ \hline\end{array}$

16. $\begin{array}{r}2\\ \times 5\\ \hline\end{array}$ 17. $\begin{array}{r}2\\ \times 7\\ \hline\end{array}$ 18. $\begin{array}{r}6\\ \times 1\\ \hline\end{array}$ 19. $\begin{array}{r}2\\ \times 4\\ \hline\end{array}$ 20. $\begin{array}{r}1\\ \times 9\\ \hline\end{array}$

Use mental math. Write just the answer.

21. $5 \times 1 \times 2 = $ _____

22. $7 \times 0 \times 2 = $ _____

23. $1 \times 2 \times 8 = $ _____

24. $3 \times 2 \times 1 = $ _____

25. $4 \times 2 \times 1 = $ _____

26. $2 \times 2 \times 1 = $ _____

Name _____ Date _____

BASIC FACTS

Multiplying by 1 and 2

Multiply. Think of doubles.

1. $2 \times 3 =$ _____

2. $2 \times 5 =$ _____

3. $2 \times 4 =$ _____

4. $2 \times 9 =$ _____

5. $2 \times 2 =$ _____

6. $2 \times 8 =$ _____

Multiply.

7. $1 \times 4 =$ _____

8. $1 \times 8 =$ _____

9. $6 \times 2 =$ _____

10. $9 \times 1 =$ _____

11. $1 \times 3 =$ _____

12. $2 \times 2 =$ _____

13. $1 \times 5 =$ _____

14. $7 \times 2 =$ _____

15. $2 \times 9 =$ _____

16. $\begin{array}{r} 1 \\ \times\, 2 \\ \hline \end{array}$

17. $\begin{array}{r} 7 \\ \times\, 1 \\ \hline \end{array}$

18. $\begin{array}{r} 5 \\ \times\, 2 \\ \hline \end{array}$

19. $\begin{array}{r} 1 \\ \times\, 9 \\ \hline \end{array}$

20. $\begin{array}{r} 2 \\ \times\, 1 \\ \hline \end{array}$

21. $\begin{array}{r} 1 \\ \times\, 1 \\ \hline \end{array}$

22. $\begin{array}{r} 1 \\ \times\, 6 \\ \hline \end{array}$

23. $\begin{array}{r} 8 \\ \times\, 2 \\ \hline \end{array}$

24. $\begin{array}{r} 1 \\ \times\, 4 \\ \hline \end{array}$

25. $\begin{array}{r} 2 \\ \times\, 6 \\ \hline \end{array}$

26. $\begin{array}{r} 8 \\ \times\, 1 \\ \hline \end{array}$

27. $\begin{array}{r} 1 \\ \times\, 3 \\ \hline \end{array}$

28. $\begin{array}{r} 3 \\ \times\, 2 \\ \hline \end{array}$

29. $\begin{array}{r} 2 \\ \times\, 7 \\ \hline \end{array}$

30. $\begin{array}{r} 4 \\ \times\, 2 \\ \hline \end{array}$

Name_____ Date _____

BASIC FACTS

Multiplying by 4

Write one addition sentence and one multiplication sentence to describe each array.

1. • • • •
   • • • •

2. • • •
   • • •
   • • •
   • • •

_____ = _____

_____ = _____

_____ = _____

_____ = _____

Multiply.

3. $4 \times 3 =$ _____

4. $4 \times 8 =$ _____

5. $7 \times 4 =$ _____

6. $5 \times 4 =$ _____

7. $4 \times 2 =$ _____

8. $4 \times 4 =$ _____

9. 4
    $\times 7$

10. 4
    $\times 4$

11. 4
    $\times 3$

12. 9
    $\times 4$

13. 5
    $\times 4$

14. 4
    $\times 6$

15. 3
    $\times 4$

16. 7
    $\times 4$

17. 4
    $\times 8$

18. 2
    $\times 4$

Name_____ Date _____

 # BASIC FACTS

Multiplying by 4

Multiply. Think of doubles or the order property.

1. 2 × 7 = _____   **2.** 6 × 2 = _____   **3.** 2 × 9 = _____

4. 4 × 2 = _____   **5.** 2 × 8 = _____   **6.** 2 × 5 = _____

7. 2 × 3 = _____   **8.** 9 × 2 = _____   **9.** 2 × 2 = _____

Multiply.

10. 4 × 3 = _____   **11.** 4 × 8 = _____   **12.** 7 × 4 = _____

13. 5 × 4 = _____   **14.** 4 × 2 = _____   **15.** 4 × 4 = _____

16. 9 × 4 = _____   **17.** 4 × 6 = _____   **18.** 8 × 4 = _____

19. 1 × 4 = _____   **20.** 2 × 4 = _____   **21.** 6 × 4 = _____

22. 4 × 7 = _____   **23.** 4 × 1 = _____   **24.** 4 × 9 = _____

25. 3 × 4 = _____   **26.** 4 × 5= _____   **27.** 4 × 6 = _____

28. 4 × 8 = _____   **29.** 4 × 2 = _____   **30.** 7 × 4 = _____

Name_____ Date _____

BASIC FACTS

Multiplying by 3

Multiply.

1. 2 ×3	**2.** 5 ×3	**3.** 6 ×3	**4.** 4 ×3
5. 9 ×3	**6.** 8 ×3	**7.** 7 ×3	**8.** 3 ×3
9. 3 ×9	**10.** 3 ×5	**11.** 3 ×6	**12.** 3 ×2

Think of multiplication facts. Complete the tables.

	x	2
13.	6	12
14.	7	
15.	3	
16.	4	
17.	5	

	x	3
18.		27
19.	6	
20.		12
21.		24
22.		15

Name_____ Date _____

BASIC FACTS

Multiplying by 3

Match.

1. $3 \times 4 = $ _____   **a.** 9×1

2. $3 \times 5 = $ _____   **b.** 9×2

3. $3 \times 6 = $ _____   **c.** 6×2

4. $7 \times 3 = $ _____   **d.** 5×3

5. $3 \times 2 = $ _____   **e.** 1×3

6. $3 \times 3 = $ _____   **f.** 3×7

7. $3 \times 1 = $ _____   **g.** 6×1

Write pairs of factors for each product.

8. _____ $\times$ _____ $= 4$ **9.** _____ $\times$ _____ $= 8$

10. _____ $\times$ _____ $= 3$ **11.** _____ $\times$ _____ $= 5$

12. _____ $\times$ _____ $= 6$ **13.** _____ $\times$ _____ $= 10$

14. _____ $\times$ _____ $= 7$ **15.** _____ $\times$ _____ $= 9$

16. _____ $\times$ _____ $= 12$ **17.** _____ $\times$ _____ $= 15$

Name_____ Date _____

BASIC FACTS

··

Multiplying by 6

Multiply.

1. 3 $\times$ 6	**2.** 5 $\times$ 6	**3.** 6 $\times$ 2	**4.** 4 $\times$ 6	**5.** 0 $\times$ 6
6. 1 $\times$ 6	**7.** 6 $\times$ 4	**8.** 9 $\times$ 6	**9.** 8 $\times$ 6	**10.** 6 $\times$ 2

Compare. Write <, >, or =.

11. 5×6 _____ 3×6 **12.** 4×3 _____ 2×6

13. 3×3 _____ 6×2 **14.** 3×2 _____ 6×1

Multiply.

15. $6 \times 3 =$ _____   **16.** $6 \times 0 =$ _____   **17.** $9 \times 6 =$ _____

18. $5 \times 6 =$ _____   **19.** $6 \times 1 =$ _____   **20.** $7 \times 6 =$ _____

21. $2 \times 6 =$ _____   **22.** $6 \times 4 =$ _____   **23.** $6 \times 6 =$ _____

24. $6 \times 8 =$ _____   **25.** $3 \times 6 =$ _____   **26.** $6 \times 5 =$ _____

Name_____ Date _____

BASIC FACTS

....

Multiplying by 6

**Draw an array for each multiplication sentence.
Find the product.**

1. $6 \times 3 =$ _____   **2.** $2 \times 6 =$ _____

Multiply.

3. 6 $\times 6$	**4.** 6 $\times 4$	**5.** 9 $\times 6$	**6.** 3 $\times 6$	**7.** 6 $\times 2$
8. 7 $\times 6$	**9.** 8 $\times 6$	**10.** 4 $\times 6$	**11.** 0 $\times 6$	**12.** 6 $\times 8$
13. 2 $\times 9$	**14.** 5 $\times 6$	**15.** 8 $\times 3$	**16.** 6 $\times 1$	**17.** 3 $\times 2$

         Grade 4, Just the Facts

Name_____ Date _____

BASIC FACTS
....
Multiplying by 5

Multiply.

1. $\begin{array}{r} 3 \\ \times\, 5 \\ \hline \end{array}$	**2.** $\begin{array}{r} 5 \\ \times\, 6 \\ \hline \end{array}$	**3.** $\begin{array}{r} 7 \\ \times\, 5 \\ \hline \end{array}$	**4.** $\begin{array}{r} 2 \\ \times\, 5 \\ \hline \end{array}$	**5.** $\begin{array}{r} 5 \\ \times\, 8 \\ \hline \end{array}$
6. $\begin{array}{r} 5 \\ \times\, 4 \\ \hline \end{array}$	**7.** $\begin{array}{r} 9 \\ \times\, 5 \\ \hline \end{array}$	**8.** $\begin{array}{r} 6 \\ \times\, 5 \\ \hline \end{array}$	**9.** $\begin{array}{r} 8 \\ \times\, 5 \\ \hline \end{array}$	**10.** $\begin{array}{r} 5 \\ \times\, 9 \\ \hline \end{array}$

Compare. Write < or >.

11. 5×6 _____ 3×6 　　　　　**12.** 5×7 _____ 9×5

13. 5×8 _____ $5 + 8$ 　　　　　**14.** 5×9 _____ 4×8

Complete the multiplication table.

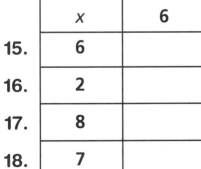

	x	6
15.	6	
16.	2	
17.	8	
18.	7	
19.	9	

Name_____ Date _____

BASIC FACTS

Multiplying by 5

Multiply.

1. $5 \times 2 =$ _____

2. $3 \times 5 =$ _____

3. $4 \times 5 =$ _____

$2 \times 5 =$ _____

$5 \times 3 =$ _____

$5 \times 4 =$ _____

Find the products. Write whether each product is *greater than*, *less than*, or *equal to* 40.

4. $8 \times 5 =$ _____   _____

5. $5 \times 6 =$ _____   _____

6. $2 \times 5 =$ _____   _____

7. $9 \times 5 =$ _____   _____

8. $5 \times 10 =$ _____   _____

Multiply.

9. $8 \times 5 =$ _____

10. $5 \times 3 =$ _____

11. $8 \times 2 =$ _____

12. $9 \times 5 =$ _____

13. $4 \times 5 =$ _____

14. $6 \times 5 =$ _____

15. $0 \times 5 =$ _____

16. $7 \times 5 =$ _____

17. $5 \times 2 =$ _____

Name_____ Date _____

BASIC FACTS
....
Multiplying by 9

**Complete the multiplication table. Use the table
to complete the number sentences.**

x	9
1. 1	
2. 2	
3. 3	
4. 4	
5. 5	

6. 9
    × 2
    ⬚

7. 4
    × 9
    ⬚

8. 1
    × ⬚
    9

9. ⬚
    × 9
    36

Multiply.

10. 9
     × 7

11. 9
     × 4

12. 9
     × 3

13. 9
     × 2

14. 4
     × 9

15. 8
     × 9

16. 5
     × 9

17. 9
     × 9

18. 3
     × 9

19. 2
     × 9

Name_____ Date _____

BASIC FACTS

Multiplying by 9

Complete the chart below, using what you know about nines facts.

1.	1×9	=	
2.	2×9	=	
3.	3×9	=	
4.	4×9	=	
5.	5×9	=	
6.	6×9	=	
7.	7×9	=	
8.	8×9	=	
9.	9×9	=	

Multiply.

10. $\begin{array}{r} 9 \\ \times 4 \\ \hline \end{array}$ **11.** $\begin{array}{r} 9 \\ \times 6 \\ \hline \end{array}$ **12.** $\begin{array}{r} 4 \\ \times 5 \\ \hline \end{array}$ **13.** $\begin{array}{r} 7 \\ \times 6 \\ \hline \end{array}$ **14.** $\begin{array}{r} 7 \\ \times 9 \\ \hline \end{array}$

15. $9 \times 5 =$ _____   **16.** $9 \times 1 =$ _____   **17.** $0 \times 9 =$ ___

Fill in the blanks.

18. $2 \times$ ____ $= 18$ **19.** $3 \times 9 =$ ____   **20.** $9 \times$ ____ $= 9$

21. ____ $\times 9 = 36$ **22.** ____ $\times 9 = 9$ **23.** $9 \times$ ____ $= 45$

Name_____ Date _____

BASIC FACTS

Multiplying by 7

Find the products. Write whether each product is *greater than*, *less than*, or *equal to* 30.

1. $7 \times 3 =$ _____

2. $7 \times 8 =$ _____

3. $6 \times 7 =$ _____

4. $5 \times 7 =$ _____

Multiply.

5. 3 $\times 7$	**6.** 4 $\times 7$	**7.** 7 $\times 6$	**8.** 5 $\times 7$	**9.** 7 $\times 5$
10. 8 $\times 7$	**11.** 2 $\times 7$	**12.** 1 $\times 7$	**13.** 0 $\times 7$	**14.** 9 $\times 7$

Use estimation. Write < or >.

15. $7 \times 3 = 21$, so 7×4 ____ 21

16. $7 \times 2 = 14$, so 7×1 ____ 14

17. $7 \times 5 = 35$, so 7×4 ____ 35

18. $7 \times 6 = 42$, so 7×7 ____ 42

Name_____ Date _____

BASIC FACTS

Multiplying by 7

Multiply.

	x	7
1.	8	
2.	3	
3.	9	
4.	6	
5.	7	

6. $7 \times 7 =$ _____

7. $6 \times 8 =$ _____

8. $1 \times 7 =$ _____

9. $8 \times 7 =$ _____

10. $7 \times 4 =$ _____

11. $7 \times 3 =$ _____

12. $4 \times 7 =$ _____

13. $6 \times 7 =$ _____

14. $7 \times 9 =$ _____

15. $7 \times 8 =$ _____

16. $3 \times 9 =$ _____

17. $2 \times 7 =$ _____

Multiply and add using mental math. Work from left to right. Write just the answer.

18. $7 \times 8 + 3 =$ _____

19. $7 \times 4 + 2 =$ _____

20. $2 \times 7 + 4 =$ _____

21. $3 \times 7 + 3 =$ _____

Name_____ Date _____

BASIC FACTS

Multiplying by 8

Multiply.

1. 8 × 6	**2.** 8 × 7	**3.** 8 × 3	**4.** 6 × 8	**5.** 5 × 8

6. 7 × 8	**7.** 8 × 4	**8.** 0 × 8	**9.** 8 × 8	**10.** 1 × 8

Complete the table.

	x	8
11.	2	
12.		64
13.	7	
14.	4	
15.		40

Multiply and add using mental math. Work from left to right. Write just the answer.

16. $5 \times 8 + 2 =$ _____   **17.** $1 \times 8 + 4 =$ _____

18. $8 \times 2 + 2 =$ _____   **19.** $3 \times 8 + 1 =$ _____

Name_____ Date _____

BASIC FACTS

Multiplying by 8

Multiply.

1. $8 \times 7 =$ _____

2. $8 \times 5 =$ _____

3. $8 \times 3 =$ _____

4. $1 \times 8 =$ _____

5. $4 \times 8 =$ _____

6. $8 \times 2 =$ _____

7. $8 \times 4 =$ _____

8. $8 \times 1 =$ _____

9. $6 \times 8 =$ _____

Complete the table with the facts you have learned. One column has been completed for you.

	x	2	3	4	5	6	7	8	9
10.	2			8					
11.	3			12					
12.	4			16					
13.	5			20					
14.	6			24					
15.	7			28					
16.	8			32					
17.	9			36					

Compare. Write <, >, or =.

18. 2×8 ___ 3×5

19. 3×8 ___ 4×8

20. 8×4 ___ 5×9

21. 4×6 ___ 3×8

22. 2×8 ___ 3×5

23. 1×8 ___ $1 + 8$

Name_____   Date _____

BASIC FACTS

Using Arrays

Write two multiplication facts.

1. • • • •
• • • •
• • • •

_____

_____

2. • • • • • •
• • • • • •
• • • • • •

_____

_____

3. • • • • •
• • • • •
• • • • •

_____

_____

Use the order property. Complete.

4. 4 × 5 = _____ × _____

5. 2 × 6 = _____ × _____

6. 7 × 3 = _____ × _____

7. 8 × 2 = _____ × _____

Write a multiplication fact.

8. 3 sevens = _____

9. 5 fives = _____

Write a division number sentence.

10. • • • • • •
• • • • • •

_____

11. • • • • •
• • • • •
• • • • •

_____

Name_____ Date _____

BASIC FACTS

Using Arrays

Draw an array. Then multiply.

1. 2
   × 3

2. 4
   × 4

3. 3
   × 6

4. 2
   × 8

5. 5
   × 3

6. 4
   × 2

7. 2
   × 7

8. 3
   × 4

9. 5
   × 2

10. 2
   × 6

11. 3
   × 3

12. 5
   × 4

Draw an array. Then divide.

13. 8 ÷ 2 = _____

14. 15 ÷ 3 = _____

15. 6 ÷ 3 = _____

16. 18 ÷ 3 = _____

17. 6 ÷ 2 = _____

18. 18 ÷ 2 = _____

19. 10 ÷ 2 = _____

20. 12 ÷ 3 = _____

21. 16 ÷ 2 = _____

Name_____ Date _____

BASIC FACTS

Multiplying and Dividing by 2

Look at the multiplication sentences below. Write a related division fact for each.

1. 2 × 2 = 4 _____

2. 2 × 5 = 10 _____

3. 2 × 6 = 12 _____

List the first ten multiples.

4. of 2 ____ ____ ____ ____ ____ ____ ____ ____ ____ ____

Draw a picture of the groups in the division fact.

5. 8 ÷ 2   **6.** 14 ÷ 2

Write the correct sign. Choose +, ×, or ÷.

7. 45 ___ 5 = 9   **8.** 4 ___ 3 = 12   **9.** 9 ___ 9 = 18

Write a multiplication sentence. Then solve.

10. 8 ÷ 4 = ____ _____   **11.** 5 ÷ 5 = ____ _____

12. 2 ÷ 1 = ____ _____   **13.** 14 ÷ 7 = ____ _____

Name_____ Date _____

BASIC FACTS

Multiplying and Dividing by 2

Multiply. Think of doubles or the order property.

1. $2 \times 7 =$ _____

2. $6 \times 2 =$ _____

3. $2 \times 9 =$ _____

4. $4 \times 2 =$ _____

5. $2 \times 8 =$ _____

6. $2 \times 5 =$ _____

7. $2 \times 3 =$ _____

8. $1 \times 2 =$ _____

9. $2 \times 2 =$ _____

10. $\begin{array}{r} 2 \\ \times\, 5 \\ \hline \end{array}$
11. $\begin{array}{r} 2 \\ \times\, 3 \\ \hline \end{array}$
12. $\begin{array}{r} 8 \\ \times\, 2 \\ \hline \end{array}$
13. $\begin{array}{r} 9 \\ \times\, 2 \\ \hline \end{array}$
14. $\begin{array}{r} 2 \\ \times\, 4 \\ \hline \end{array}$
15. $\begin{array}{r} 2 \\ \times\, 6 \\ \hline \end{array}$

Divide.

16. $8 \div 2 =$ _____

17. $6 \div 2 =$ _____

18. $18 \div 2 =$ _____

19. $10 \div 2 =$ _____

20. $16 \div 2 =$ _____

21. $12 \div 2 =$ _____

22. $14 \div 2 =$ _____

23. $2 \div 1 =$ _____

24. $4 \div 2 =$ _____

Write a division sentence. Then solve.

25. $2 \times 7 =$ ____ _____

26. $2 \times 3 =$ ____ _____

27. $2 \times 4 =$ ____ _____

28. $2 \times 8 =$ ____ _____

Name_____ Date _____

BASIC FACTS

Multiplying and Dividing by 4

Find the missing factor. Complete.

1. $9 \times$ _____ $= 36$　　　　**2.** $4 \times$ _____ $= 32$　　　　**3.** $4 \times$ _____ $= 12$

4. $7 \times 4 = 4 \times$ _____　　**5.** $4 \times 5 = 5 \times$ _____　　**6.** _____ $\times 7 = 28$

7. $4 \times$ _____ $= 16$　　　　**8.** $2 \times$ _____ $= 4 \times 2$　　**9.** $4 \times$ _____ $= 24$

List the first ten multiples.

10. of 4 _____ _____ _____ _____ _____ _____ _____ _____ _____ _____

Write a related multiplication fact. Then divide.

11. $10 \div 2 =$ _____　　　　**12.** $8 \div 4 =$ _____　　　　**13.** $16 \div 4 =$ _____

_____　　　　_____　　　　_____

14. $14 \div 2 =$ _____　　　　**15.** $24 \div 4 =$ _____　　　　**16.** $20 \div 4 =$ _____

_____　　　　_____　　　　_____

17. $32 \div 4 =$ _____　　　　**18.** $18 \div 2 =$ _____　　　　**19.** $28 \div 4 =$ _____

_____　　　　_____　　　　_____

Name_____ Date _____

BASIC FACTS

Multiplying and Dividing by 4

Divide. Check by multiplying.

1. 4)$\overline{8}$

_____

2. 4)$\overline{32}$

_____

3. 4)$\overline{24}$

_____

4. 4)$\overline{16}$

_____

5. 4)$\overline{36}$

_____

6. 4)$\overline{12}$

_____

7. $28 \div 4 =$ _____

_____

8. $20 \div 4 =$ _____

_____

9. $12 \div 4 =$ _____

_____

Multiply.

10. 6
     $\times\,4$

11. 5
     $\times\,4$

12. 7
     $\times\,4$

13. 4
     $\times\,8$

14. 4
     $\times\,9$

15. 3
     $\times\,4$

16. 4
     $\times\,4$

17. 9
     $\times\,4$

18. 8
     $\times\,4$

19. 4
     $\times\,5$

20. $4 \times 3 =$ _____

21. $2 \times 7 =$ _____

22. $6 \times 4 =$ _____

Name_____ Date _____

BASIC FACTS

Multiplying and Dividing by 5

Multiply.

1. $5 \times (1 \times 8) =$ _____

2. $(3 \times 5) \times 1 =$ _____

3. $5 \times 2 =$ _____

4. $5 \times 5 =$ _____

5. $5 \times 8 =$ _____

6. $5 \times 9 =$ _____

Complete.

7. $6 \times (1 \times 5) =$ _____

8. $1 \times 5 \times 6 =$ _____

List the first ten multiples.

9. of 5 ____ ____ ____ ____ ____ ____ ____ ____ ____ ____

Divide. Think of multiplication.

10. $40 \div 5 =$ _____

11. $35 \div 5 =$ _____

12. $25 \div 5 =$ _____

13. $10 \div 5 =$ _____

14. $20 \div 5 =$ _____

15. $30 \div 5 =$ _____

16. $15 \div 5 =$ _____

17. $45 \div 5 =$ _____

18. $5 \div 1 =$ _____

19. $40 \div 8 =$ _____

20. $35 \div 7 =$ _____

21. $45 \div 9 =$ _____

Name_____ Date _____

BASIC FACTS

Multiplying and Dividing by 5

What is the quotient? Think of multiplication.

1. 5)‾25‾   2. 5)‾30‾   3. 5)‾45‾   4. 5)‾40‾

5. 5)‾35‾   6. 5)‾50‾   7. 5)‾15‾   8. 5)‾20‾

List the multiples

9. of 4 up to 50

_____

Complete the number sentence.

10. 45 = ____ × ____   11. 25 ÷ 5 = ____   12. ____ = 7 × 5

13. 5 × 8 = ____   14. 3 × 7 = ____   15. 18 = ____ × 2

16. 54 = ____ × ____   17. 20 = ____ × ____   18. 50 ÷ ____ = 10

19. 30 = ____ × ____   20. 10 ÷ 2 = ____   21. ____ ÷ 5 = 9

22. 15 ÷ 5 = ____   23. 6 × 4 = ____   24. 9 ÷ 3 = ____

Name_____ Date _____

BASIC FACTS
···
Multiplying and Dividing by 1

Use multiplication and division properties to complete.

1. 8 ÷ _____ = 1   **2.** (6 × 2) × 1 = 1 × _____

3. (3 × _____) × 5 = 1 × (3 × 5)   **4.** _____ ÷ 1 = 10

Multiply.

5. 1	**6.** 7	**7.** 5	**8.** 1	**9.** 2	**10.** 1
× 2	× 1	× 1	× 9	× 1	× 1

11. 1	**12.** 8	**13.** 1	**14.** 6	**15.** 1	**16.** 1
× 6	× 1	× 4	× 1	× 7	× 3

Write a multiplication sentence. Then solve.

17. 5 ÷ 5 = ____ _____   **18.** 3 ÷ 1 = ____ _____

What is the quotient? Think of multiplication.

19. 1)‾5   **20.** 1)‾1   **21.** 1)‾8   **22.** 1)‾3

Name_____ Date _____

BASIC FACTS

Multiplying and Dividing by 1

Multiply.

1. $1 \times 4 =$ _____   **2.** $1 \times 8 =$ _____   **3.** $6 \times 2 =$ _____

4. $9 \times 1 =$ _____   **5.** $1 \times 3 =$ _____   **6.** $2 \times 4 =$ _____

7. $1 \times 5 =$ _____   **8.** $7 \times 1 =$ _____   **9.** $2 \times 9 =$ _____

10. $\begin{array}{r} 2 \\ \times\,2 \\ \hline \end{array}$ **11.** $\begin{array}{r} 1 \\ \times\,7 \\ \hline \end{array}$ **12.** $\begin{array}{r} 5 \\ \times\,4 \\ \hline \end{array}$ **13.** $\begin{array}{r} 1 \\ \times\,9 \\ \hline \end{array}$ **14.** $\begin{array}{r} 2 \\ \times\,1 \\ \hline \end{array}$

15. $\begin{array}{r} 1 \\ \times\,2 \\ \hline \end{array}$ **16.** $\begin{array}{r} 1 \\ \times\,6 \\ \hline \end{array}$ **17.** $\begin{array}{r} 8 \\ \times\,4 \\ \hline \end{array}$ **18.** $\begin{array}{r} 4 \\ \times\,1 \\ \hline \end{array}$ **19.** $\begin{array}{r} 2 \\ \times\,7 \\ \hline \end{array}$

Divide.

20. $4 \div 1 =$ _____   **21.** $6 \div 1 =$ _____   **22.** $2 \div 1 =$ _____

23. $18 \div 2 =$ _____   **24.** $12 \div 1 =$ _____   **25.** $24 \div 3 =$ _____

26. $25 \div 5 =$ _____   **27.** $24 \div 4 =$ _____   **28.** $8 \div 1 =$ _____

29. $40 \div 5 =$ _____   **30.** $11 \div 1 =$ _____   **31.** $16 \div 4 =$ _____

BASIC FACTS

Multiplying and Dividing by 3

Complete each fact family.

1. 3 × 2 = _____   6 ÷ 2 = _____

   2 × 3 = _____   6 ÷ 3 = _____

2. 6 × 3 = _____   18 ÷ 6 = _____

   3 × 6 = _____   18 ÷ 3 = _____

3. 8 × 3 = _____   24 ÷ 3 = _____

   3 × 8 = _____   24 ÷ 8 = _____

4. 3 × 9 = _____   27 ÷ 9 = _____

   9 × 3 = _____   27 ÷ 3 = _____

5. 5 × 3 = _____   15 ÷ 3 = _____

   3 × 5 = _____   15 ÷ 5 = _____

Write four number sentences for each fact family.

6. 3, 4, 12 _____ _____ _____ _____

7. 3, 7, 21 _____ _____ _____ _____

Name_____ Date _____

BASIC FACTS

···

Multiplying and Dividing by 3

Write a related multiplication fact. Then divide.

1. 6 ÷ 3 = ____

___ × ___ = ___

2. 21 ÷ 3 = ____

___ × ___ = ___

3. 12 ÷ 3 = ____

___ × ___ = ___

4. 3 ÷ 3 = ____

___ × ___ = ___

5. 9 ÷ 3 = ____

___ × ___ = ___

6. 24 ÷ 3 = ____

___ × ___ = ___

7. 15 ÷ 3 = ____

___ × ___ = ___

8. 0 ÷ 3 = ____

___ × ___ = ___

9. 18 ÷ 3 = ____

___ × ___ = ___

10. 27 ÷ 3 = ____

___ × ___ = ___

Check by multiplying. Correct any mistakes.

11. 12 ÷ 3 = 6

_____

12. 9 ÷ 3 = 3

_____

13. 15 ÷ 3 = 4

_____

Name_____ Date _____

BASIC FACTS

Reviewing 1's - 5's and 0's

Multiply.

1. $0 \times 4 =$ _____

2. $1 \times 8 =$ _____

3. $6 \times 0 =$ _____

4. $9 \times 1 =$ _____

5. $0 \times 3 =$ _____

6. $2 \times 0 =$ _____

7. $1 \times 5 =$ _____

8. $7 \times 0 =$ _____

9. $0 \times 9 =$ _____

10. $\begin{array}{r} 7 \\ \times\, 1 \\ \hline \end{array}$

11. $\begin{array}{r} 5 \\ \times\, 5 \\ \hline \end{array}$

12. $\begin{array}{r} 3 \\ \times\, 0 \\ \hline \end{array}$

13. $\begin{array}{r} 2 \\ \times\, 1 \\ \hline \end{array}$

14. $\begin{array}{r} 1 \\ \times\, 0 \\ \hline \end{array}$

15. $\begin{array}{r} 8 \\ \times\, 0 \\ \hline \end{array}$

16. $\begin{array}{r} 1 \\ \times\, 4 \\ \hline \end{array}$

17. $\begin{array}{r} 1 \\ \times\, 3 \\ \hline \end{array}$

18. $\begin{array}{r} 6 \\ \times\, 2 \\ \hline \end{array}$

19. $\begin{array}{r} 2 \\ \times\, 7 \\ \hline \end{array}$

20. $\begin{array}{r} 3 \\ \times\, 3 \\ \hline \end{array}$

21. $\begin{array}{r} 3 \\ \times\, 7 \\ \hline \end{array}$

22. $\begin{array}{r} 8 \\ \times\, 3 \\ \hline \end{array}$

23. $\begin{array}{r} 3 \\ \times\, 5 \\ \hline \end{array}$

24. $\begin{array}{r} 4 \\ \times\, 3 \\ \hline \end{array}$

25. $\begin{array}{r} 2 \\ \times\, 5 \\ \hline \end{array}$

26. $\begin{array}{r} 5 \\ \times\, 4 \\ \hline \end{array}$

27. $\begin{array}{r} 2 \\ \times\, 4 \\ \hline \end{array}$

28. $\begin{array}{r} 4 \\ \times\, 4 \\ \hline \end{array}$

29. $\begin{array}{r} 5 \\ \times\, 0 \\ \hline \end{array}$

Name_____ Date _____

BASIC FACTS

Reviewing 1's - 5's and 0's

Find the quotient. Think of multiplication.

1. 1)5   **2.** 5)0   **3.** 1)4   **4.** 8)0

5. 7)14   **6.** 9)0   **7.** 1)9   **8.** 8)8

9. 3)15   **10.** 1)8   **11.** 1)3   **12.** 6)0

13. 6)6   **14.** 2)0   **15.** 4)16   **16.** 1)7

Write a multiplication sentence. Then solve.

17. $0 \div 4 =$ _____ _____   **18.** $5 \div 5 =$ _____ _____

19. $3 \div 1 =$ _____ _____   **20.** $10 \div 2 =$ _____ _____

21. $6 \div 3 =$ _____ _____   **22.** $0 \div 3 =$ _____ _____

23. $8 \div 1 =$ _____ _____   **24.** $14 \div 2 =$ _____ _____

25. $4 \div 1 =$ _____ _____   **26.** $9 \div 3 =$ _____ _____

27. $3 \div 3 =$ _____ _____   **28.** $16 \div 1 =$ _____ _____

Name_____ Date _____

BASIC FACTS

Multiplying by 9

Find two multiplication facts.

1. • • • • • • • • •
   • • • • • • • • •
   • • • • • • • • •

   _____

   _____

2. • • • • • • • • •
   • • • • • • • • •

   _____

   _____

Find the missing factor. Complete.

3. ____ × 3 = 27   4. 9 × ____ = 72   5. 6 × 9 = 9 × ____

Complete the number sentence.

6. 36 = ____ × ____   7. 18 = ____ × ____   8. 45 = ____ × ____

Multiply.

9. 5   10. 7   11. 3   12. 4   13. 9
  × 9   × 9   × 9   × 9   × 9

14. 6   15. 9   16. 2   17. 1   18. 8
  × 9   × 5   × 9   × 9   × 9

Name_____ Date _____

BASIC FACTS

Dividing by 9

Divide.

1. $0 \div 9 =$ _____

2. $9 \div 1 =$ _____

3. $5 \div 1 =$ _____

4. $9 \div 9 =$ _____

5. $54 \div 6 =$ _____

6. $27 \div 9 =$ _____

7. $9 \div 3 =$ _____

8. $18 \div 9 =$ _____

9. $45 \div 9 =$ _____

10. $63 \div 9 =$ _____

11. $36 \div 9 =$ _____

12. $81 \div 9 =$ _____

13. $72 \div 9 =$ _____

14. $27 \div 9 =$ _____

15. $54 \div 9 =$ _____

Compare. Write >, <, or =.

16. $18 \div 2$ _____ $18 \div 9$

17. $9 \div 9$ _____ $3 \div 3$

18. $27 \div 9$ _____ $25 \div 5$

19. $24 \div 6$ _____ $36 \div 4$

Divide.

20. $2\overline{)18}$

21. $9\overline{)81}$

22. $9\overline{)27}$

23. $9\overline{)9}$

24. $9\overline{)36}$

25. $6\overline{)54}$

26. $5\overline{)45}$

27. $8\overline{)72}$

Name_____ Date _____

BASIC FACTS

Multiplying by 6

Multiply.

1. 3 × 3 = _____   6 × 3 = _____   **2.** 3 × 2 = _____   6 × 2 = _____

3. 3 × 7 = _____   6 × 7 = _____   **4.** 3 × 4 = _____   6 × 4 = _____

5. 3 × 9 = _____   6 × 9 = _____   **6.** 3 × 5 = _____   6 × 5 = _____

7. 3 × 8 = _____   6 × 8 = _____   **8.** 3 × 6 = _____   6 × 6 = _____

9. 4 × 6	**10.** 3 × 6	**11.** 5 × 6	**12.** 7 × 6	**13.** 6 × 6
14. 6 × 1	**15.** 2 × 6	**16.** 6 × 0	**17.** 9 × 6	**18.** 8 × 6
19. 6 × 5	**20.** 6 × 7	**21.** 6 × 4	**22.** 6 × 3	**23.** 7 × 3
24. 6 × 2	**25.** 6 × 8	**26.** 6 × 9	**27.** 5 × 5	**28.** 8 × 2

Name_____ Date _____

BASIC FACTS

Multiplying and Dividing by 6

Write four number sentences for each fact family.

1. 6, 7, 42

_____ × _____ = _____

_____ × _____ = _____

_____ ÷ _____ = _____

_____ ÷ _____ = _____

2. 5, 6, 30

_____ × _____ = _____

_____ × _____ = _____

_____ ÷ _____ = _____

_____ ÷ _____ = _____

3. 6, 8, 48

_____ × _____ = _____

_____ × _____ = _____

_____ ÷ _____ = _____

_____ ÷ _____ = _____

4. 6, 9, 54

_____ × _____ = _____

_____ × _____ = _____

_____ ÷ _____ = _____

_____ ÷ _____ = _____

5. 4, 6, 24

_____ × _____ = _____

_____ × _____ = _____

_____ ÷ _____ = _____

_____ ÷ _____ = _____

Name_____   Date _____

BASIC FACTS
....
Multiplying and Dividing by 7

Write a related multiplication fact. Then divide.

1. 7 ÷ 7 = ___

___ × ___ = ___

2. 21 ÷ 7 = ___

___ × ___ = ___

3. 35 ÷ 7 = ___

___ × ___ = ___

4. 56 ÷ 7 = ___

___ × ___ = ___

5. 42 ÷ 7 = ___

___ × ___ = ___

6. 63 ÷ 7 = ___

___ × ___ = ___

7. 14 ÷ 7 = ___

___ × ___ = ___

8. 28 ÷ 7 = ___

___ × ___ = ___

9. 49 ÷ 7 = ___

___ × ___ = ___

Write four number sentences for each fact family.

10. 7, 9, 63

_____ × _____ = _____

_____ × _____ = _____

_____ ÷ _____ = _____

_____ ÷ _____ = _____

11. 7, 8, 56

_____ × _____ = _____

_____ × _____ = _____

_____ ÷ _____ = _____

_____ ÷ _____ = _____

Name_____   Date _____

BASIC FACTS

Multiplying and Dividing by 7

Multiply.

1. $7 \times 2 =$ _____

2. $7 \times 5 =$ _____

3. $7 \times 7 =$ _____

4. $7 \times 4 =$ _____

5. $7 \times 3 =$ _____

6. $7 \times 8 =$ _____

7. $7 \times 9 =$ _____

8. $7 \times 6 =$ _____

9. $7 \times 1 =$ _____

10. $\begin{array}{r} 7 \\ \times\,0 \\ \hline \end{array}$

11. $\begin{array}{r} 2 \\ \times\,7 \\ \hline \end{array}$

12. $\begin{array}{r} 6 \\ \times\,7 \\ \hline \end{array}$

13. $\begin{array}{r} 8 \\ \times\,7 \\ \hline \end{array}$

14. $\begin{array}{r} 4 \\ \times\,7 \\ \hline \end{array}$

15. $\begin{array}{r} 1 \\ \times\,7 \\ \hline \end{array}$

16. $\begin{array}{r} 9 \\ \times\,7 \\ \hline \end{array}$

17. $\begin{array}{r} 5 \\ \times\,7 \\ \hline \end{array}$

18. $\begin{array}{r} 7 \\ \times\,7 \\ \hline \end{array}$

19. $\begin{array}{r} 3 \\ \times\,7 \\ \hline \end{array}$

20. $\begin{array}{r} 0 \\ \times\,7 \\ \hline \end{array}$

21. $\begin{array}{r} 7 \\ \times\,1 \\ \hline \end{array}$

Divide.

22. $63 \div 7 =$ ____

23. $21 \div 7 =$ ____

24. $7 \div 7 =$ ____

25. $14 \div 7 =$ ____

26. $56 \div 7 =$ ____

27. $42 \div 7 =$ ____

28. $28 \div 7 =$ ____

29. $49 \div 7 =$ ____

30. $35 \div 7 =$ ____

Name_____ Date _____

BASIC FACTS

Multiplying by 8

Find two multiplication facts.

1. • • • • • • • •
• • • • • • • •
• • • • • • • •

_____

_____

2. • • • • • • • •
• • • • • • • •

_____

_____

3. • • • • • • • •
• • • • • • • •
• • • • • • • •
• • • • • • • •

_____

_____

Write a multiplication fact.

4. 6 eights = _____

5. 5 eights = _____

6. 7 eights = _____

7. 9 eights = _____

8. 4 eights = _____

9. 8 eights = _____

Draw an array. Find the product.

10. $6 \times 8 = $ _____

11. $3 \times 8 = $ _____

Multiply.

12. $\begin{array}{r} 6 \\ \times\ 8 \\ \hline \end{array}$

13. $\begin{array}{r} 8 \\ \times\ 5 \\ \hline \end{array}$

14. $\begin{array}{r} 7 \\ \times\ 8 \\ \hline \end{array}$

15. $\begin{array}{r} 8 \\ \times\ 4 \\ \hline \end{array}$

Name_____ Date _____

BASIC FACTS

Multiplying and Dividing by 8

Write the missing numbers.

1. ___ × 8 = 40

2. ___ × 8 = 56

3. ___ × 8 = 24

4. ___ × 8 = 64

5. ___ × 8 = 48

6. ___ × 8 = 72

7. 72 = ___ × ___

8. 56 = ___ × ___

9. 24 = ___ × ___

Divide.

10. 8)32

11. 8)16

12. 8)40

13. 8)24

14. 8)48

15. 8)8

16. 8)56

17. 8)64

Check by multiplying. Correct any quotients that are wrong.

18. 40 ÷ 8 = 6

19. 16 ÷ 8 = 3

20. 64 ÷ 8 = 7

_____

_____

_____

21. 24 ÷ 8 = 4

22. 56 ÷ 8 = 6

23. 32 ÷ 8 = 5

_____

_____

_____

Name_____ Date _____

BASIC FACTS
Review 6, 7, 8, and 9

Multiply.

1. 4 $\times\,8$	2. 9 $\times\,2$	3. 5 $\times\,8$	4. 9 $\times\,4$	5. 8 $\times\,8$
6. 9 $\times\,3$	7. 9 $\times\,7$	8. 1 $\times\,8$	9. 5 $\times\,9$	10. 7 $\times\,9$
11. 9 $\times\,9$	12. 8 $\times\,6$	13. 9 $\times\,8$	14. 3 $\times\,9$	15. 8 $\times\,7$
16. 6 $\times\,8$	17. 9 $\times\,5$	18. 2 $\times\,8$	19. 7 $\times\,7$	20. 8 $\times\,5$
21. 7 $\times\,8$	22. 3 $\times\,8$	23. 4 $\times\,9$	24. 7 $\times\,4$	25. 9 $\times\,6$
26. 6 $\times\,7$	27. 3 $\times\,9$	28. 4 $\times\,6$	29. 6 $\times\,6$	30. 2 $\times\,7$

Name_____ Date _____

BASIC FACTS

··

Review 6, 7, 8, and 9

Divide.

1. 9)36	**2.** 6)30	**3.** 8)8	**4.** 8)64	**5.** 6)24
6. 6)54	**7.** 7)42	**8.** 9)9	**9.** 8)56	**10.** 9)72
11. 7)21	**12.** 8)72	**13.** 9)45	**14.** 8)0	**15.** 6)12
16. 9)0	**17.** 9)54	**18.** 6)0	**19.** 7)49	**20.** 9)81
21. 6)36	**22.** 6)48	**23.** 7)35	**24.** 7)7	**25.** 7)28
26. 8)16	**27.** 9)18	**28.** 8)48	**29.** 8)32	**30.** 7)63
31. 6)18	**32.** 7)56	**33.** 5)30	**34.** 3)21	**35.** 8)24

Name_____ Date _____

BASIC FACTS

Review Multiplication and Division Facts

Write the fact family for each of the arrays.

1. • • • • • • • •
   • • • • • • • •
   • • • • • • • •
   • • • • • • • •

   _____ × _____ = _____

   _____ × _____ = _____

   _____ ÷ _____ = _____

   _____ ÷ _____ = _____

2. • • • • • • • •
   • • • • • • • •
   • • • • • • • •

   _____ × _____ = _____

   _____ × _____ = _____

   _____ ÷ _____ = _____

   _____ ÷ _____ = _____

Multiply.

3.

x	7
8	56
3	
9	
6	
7	

4.

x	9
3	
	63
	54
	45
9	

5.   9
   × 3
   ____

6.   4
   × 9
   ____

7.   8
   × 9
   ____

8.   5
   × 9
   ____

9.   9
   × 9
   ____

Name_____ Date _____

BASIC FACTS

Review Multiplication and Division Facts

Write four number sentences for each fact family.

1. 5, 7, 35 _____ _____ _____ _____

2. 6, 8, 48 _____ _____ _____ _____

Complete.

3. $4 \times 8 =$ _____ $32 \div 8 =$ _____

   $8 \times 4 =$ _____ $32 \div 4 =$ _____

4. $6 \times 7 =$ _____ $42 \div 7 =$ _____

   $7 \times 6 =$ _____ $42 \div 6 =$ _____

5. $8 \times 5 =$ _____ $40 \div 5 =$ _____

   $5 \times 8 =$ _____ $40 \div 8 =$ _____

6. $4 \times 9 =$ _____ $36 \div 9 =$ _____

   $9 \times 4 =$ _____ $36 \div 4 =$ _____

Divide.

7. $9\overline{)45}$ **8.** $5\overline{)40}$ **9.** $6\overline{)54}$ **10.** $7\overline{)28}$

Name_____ Date _____

BASIC FACTS: ADDITION

Find the sum. Use strategies to help you.

1. 4 + 5	**2.** 2 + 4	**3.** 0 + 7	**4.** 6 + 1	**5.** 8 + 2	**6.** 1 + 4
7. 5 + 4	**8.** 8 + 9	**9.** 6 + 5	**10.** 9 + 2	**11.** 7 + 8	**12.** 5 + 3
13. 9 + 9	**14.** 1 + 0	**15.** 3 + 5	**16.** 6 + 4	**17.** 5 + 9	**18.** 6 + 7
19. 1 + 9	**20.** 8 + 4	**21.** 1 + 5	**22.** 3 + 3	**23.** 8 + 8	**24.** 6 + 2
25. 5 + 7	**26.** 3 + 7	**27.** 3 + 9	**28.** 5 + 8	**29.** 7 + 5	**30.** 2 + 8

I need more practice with these facts:

Name_____ Date _____

BASIC FACTS: ADDITION

Find the sum. Use strategies to help you.

1.	0	2.	9	3.	7	4.	4	5.	1	6.	3
	+4		+6		+3		+5		+8		+6

7.	5	8.	2	9.	9	10.	7	11.	7	12.	4
	+0		+1		+8		+6		+4		+9

13.	4	14.	8	15.	5	16.	4	17.	1	18.	7
	+1		+5		+6		+7		+3		+9

19.	3	20.	2	21.	8	22.	9	23.	9	24.	7
	+4		+2		+7		+3		+2		+0

25.	1	26.	6	27.	5	28.	0	29.	3	30.	0
	+1		+8		+2		+6		+2		+0

I need more practice with these facts:

116   **Grade 4, Just the Facts**

Name_____ Date _____

BASIC FACTS: ADDITION

Find the sum. Use strategies to help you.

1. 4 + 3	2. 6 + 1	3. 8 + 9	4. 2 + 5	5. 2 + 0	6. 2 + 7
7. 0 + 3	8. 7 + 2	9. 5 + 5	10. 9 + 4	11. 8 + 0	12. 3 + 1
13. 6 + 6	14. 2 + 3	15. 8 + 3	16. 4 + 2	17. 6 + 9	18. 0 + 5
19. 4 + 8	20. 4 + 6	21. 2 + 9	22. 0 + 1	23. 9 + 1	24. 1 + 2
25. 5 + 1	26. 9 + 5	27. 7 + 7	28. 4 + 0	29. 9 + 7	30. 8 + 1

I need more practice with these facts:

Name_____ Date _____

BASIC FACTS: SUBTRACTION

Find the difference. Use strategies to help you.

1.	9 − 3	2.	16 − 8	3.	3 − 1	4.	7 − 6	5.	12 − 5	6.	14 − 9

| 7. | 8
− 5 | 8. | 4
− 0 | 9. | 10
− 7 | 10. | 11
− 2 | 11. | 6
− 3 | 12. | 1
− 1 |

| 13. | 7
− 1 | 14. | 8
− 8 | 15. | 9
− 4 | 16. | 5
− 5 | 17. | 16
− 7 | 18. | 10
− 6 |

| 19. | 11
− 2 | 20. | 9
− 2 | 21. | 14
− 5 | 22. | 13
− 6 | 23. | 7
− 2 | 24. | 1
− 0 |

| 25. | 9
− 8 | 26. | 5
− 4 | 27. | 18
− 9 | 28. | 12
− 8 | 29. | 6
− 2 | 30. | 15
− 8 |

I need more practice with these facts:

Name_____ Date _____

BASIC FACTS: SUBTRACTION

Find the difference. Use strategies to help you.

1. 5 − 1	2. 3 − 3	3. 9 − 0	4. 15 − 7	5. 11 − 3	6. 8 − 2
7. 9 − 7	8. 3 − 2	9. 14 − 8	10. 2 − 1	11. 6 − 4	12. 7 − 7
13. 10 − 5	14. 13 − 5	15. 8 − 0	16. 13 − 4	17. 8 − 4	18. 17 − 8
19. 2 − 0	20. 11 − 4	21. 16 − 9	22. 10 − 2	23. 7 − 3	24. 2 − 1
25. 9 − 9	26. 5 − 3	27. 12 − 7	28. 7 − 5	29. 12 − 6	30. 15 − 6

I need more practice with these facts:

Name_____ Date _____

BASIC FACTS: SUBTRACTION

Find the difference. Use strategies to help you.

1.	7 − 0	2.	4 − 3	3.	13 − 8	4.	17 − 9	5.	4 − 4	6.	11 − 7

7.	8 − 3	8.	14 − 6	9.	10 − 1	10.	0 − 0	11.	13 − 7	12.	9 − 5

13.	6 − 1	14.	11 − 5	15.	4 − 1	16.	10 − 9	17.	12 − 4	18.	3 − 0

19.	7 − 4	20.	12 − 9	21.	6 − 5	22.	8 − 1	23.	14 − 7	24.	10 − 4

25.	5 − 0	26.	12 − 3	27.	8 − 6	28.	4 − 2	29.	15 − 9	30.	8 − 7

I need more practice with these facts:

Name_____ Date _____

BASIC FACTS: MULTIPLICATION

Find the product. Use strategies to help you.

| 1. 2 ×5 | 2. 4 ×1 | 3. 8 ×7 | 4. 2 ×0 | 5. 4 ×3 | 6. 6 ×3 |

| 7. 6 ×9 | 8. 6 ×6 | 9. 0 ×6 | 10. 2 ×7 | 11. 6 ×8 | 12. 6 ×5 |

| 13. 5 ×7 | 14. 3 ×5 | 15. 4 ×7 | 16. 2 ×9 | 17. 2 ×8 | 18. 3 ×3 |

| 19. 6 ×2 | 20. 0 ×4 | 21. 7 ×9 | 22. 7 ×5 | 23. 3 ×4 | 24. 7 ×6 |

| 25. 3 ×7 | 26. 4 ×6 | 27. 8 ×5 | 28. 4 ×8 | 29. 9 ×1 | 30. 9 ×5 |

I need more practice with these facts:

Grade 4, Just the Facts

Name_____ Date _____

BASIC FACTS: MULTIPLICATION

Find the product. Use strategies to help you.

1. 0 × 8	**2.** 9 × 7	**3.** 5 × 5	**4.** 3 × 6	**5.** 2 × 1	**6.** 8 × 3
7. 4 × 3	**8.** 7 × 0	**9.** 1 × 7	**10.** 6 × 1	**11.** 8 × 8	**12.** 5 × 9
13. 9 × 2	**14.** 9 × 3	**15.** 1 × 9	**16.** 2 × 3	**17.** 0 × 0	**18.** 4 × 1
19. 7 × 7	**20.** 5 × 4	**21.** 5 × 1	**22.** 7 × 3	**23.** 9 × 6	**24.** 3 × 0
25. 3 × 6	**26.** 3 × 1	**27.** 6 × 7	**28.** 9 × 8	**29.** 2 × 6	**30.** 9 × 4

I need more practice with these facts:

Name_____ Date _____

BASIC FACTS: MULTIPLICATION

Find the product. Use strategies to help you.

1. 1 × 1	**2.** 7 × 8	**3.** 4 × 5	**4.** 9 × 2	**5.** 0 × 7	**6.** 2 × 4
7. 8 × 9	**8.** 8 × 1	**9.** 1 × 6	**10.** 5 × 2	**11.** 7 × 4	**12.** 9 × 0
13. 5 × 6	**14.** 7 × 3	**15.** 8 × 6	**16.** 3 × 4	**17.** 5 × 8	**18.** 8 × 4
19. 9 × 9	**20.** 0 × 1	**21.** 4 × 4	**22.** 0 × 5	**23.** 3 × 8	**24.** 6 × 2
25. 2 × 2	**26.** 5 × 3	**27.** 8 × 0	**28.** 3 × 9	**29.** 9 × 6	**30.** 4 × 9

I need more practice with these facts:

Name_____ Date _____

BASIC FACTS: DIVISION

Find the quotient. Use strategies to help you.

1. 1)6   2. 7)28   3. 4)12   4. 5)45   5. 3)0   6. 6)36

7. 3)27   8. 2)10   9. 8)8   10. 9)63   11. 3)21   12. 6)12

13. 5)25   14. 7)56   15. 2)2   16. 4)36   17. 5)15   18. 1)3

19. 5)35   20. 3)9   21. 1)9   22. 2)4   23. 6)0   24. 8)48

25. 9)27   26. 4)24   27. 2)14   28. 6)24   29. 4)20   30. 2)18

I need more practice with these facts:

Name_____   Date _____

BASIC FACTS: DIVISION

Find the quotient. Use strategies to help you.

1. $6\overline{)42}$ **2.** $4\overline{)32}$ **3.** $5\overline{)0}$ **4.** $1\overline{)2}$ **5.** $3\overline{)15}$ **6.** $8\overline{)64}$

7. $3\overline{)3}$ **8.** $6\overline{)18}$ **9.** $7\overline{)49}$ **10.** $3\overline{)6}$ **11.** $1\overline{)5}$ **12.** $8\overline{)40}$

13. $9\overline{)72}$ **14.** $5\overline{)30}$ **15.** $9\overline{)0}$ **16.** $4\overline{)16}$ **17.** $5\overline{)10}$ **18.** $7\overline{)21}$

19. $3\overline{)18}$ **20.** $6\overline{)6}$ **21.** $6\overline{)54}$ **22.** $2\overline{)16}$ **23.** $9\overline{)45}$ **24.** $7\overline{)14}$

25. $5\overline{)20}$ **26.** $1\overline{)0}$ **27.** $6\overline{)48}$ **28.** $4\overline{)28}$ **29.** $5\overline{)5}$ **30.** $7\overline{)35}$

I need more practice with these facts:

Grade 4, Just the Facts

BASIC FACTS: DIVISION

Find the quotient. Use strategies to help you.

1. 1)4   **2.** 7)42   **3.** 8)24   **4.** 7)7   **5.** 2)12   **6.** 8)32

7. 6)30   **8.** 4)8   **9.** 2)0   **10.** 5)40   **11.** 7)0   **12.** 3)24

13. 1)7   **14.** 8)72   **15.** 2)16   **16.** 9)9   **17.** 9)54   **18.** 2)6

19. 7)63   **20.** 4)0   **21.** 9)81   **22.** 1)1   **23.** 9)36   **24.** 8)0

25. 5)45   **26.** 3)12   **27.** 9)18   **28.** 2)8   **29.** 8)56   **30.** 4)4

I need more practice with these facts:

Practice Minutes Record

30 Minutes

Name _____

Dear Family,

Please help me practice my _____ facts.

....

I practiced:	Date	Helper
5 minutes	_____	_____
5 minutes	_____	_____
5 minutes	_____	_____
5 minutes	_____	_____
5 minutes	_____	_____
5 minutes	_____	_____

Return completed record to your teacher.

Practice Minutes Record

60 Minutes

Name _____

Dear Family,

Please help me practice my _____ facts.

....

New Facts

I practiced:	Date	Helper
5 minutes	_____	_____
5 minutes	_____	_____
5 minutes	_____	_____
5 minutes	_____	_____
5 minutes	_____	_____
5 minutes	_____	_____

Review Facts

I practiced:	Date	Helper
5 minutes	_____	_____
5 minutes	_____	_____
5 minutes	_____	_____
5 minutes	_____	_____
5 minutes	_____	_____
5 minutes	_____	_____

Return completed record to your teacher.

Practice Minutes Record

100
Minutes

Name _____

Dear Family,

Please help me practice my _____ facts.

....

New Facts

I practiced:	Date	Helper
10 minutes	_____	_____
10 minutes	_____	_____
10 minutes	_____	_____
10 minutes	_____	_____
10 minutes	_____	_____

Review Facts

I practiced:	Date	Helper
10 minutes	_____	_____
10 minutes	_____	_____
10 minutes	_____	_____
10 minutes	_____	_____
10 minutes	_____	_____

Return completed record to your teacher.

Practice Minutes Record

Name _____

Dear Family,

Please help me practice my _____ facts.

···

New Facts

I practiced:	Date	Helper
10 minutes	_____	_____
10 minutes	_____	_____
10 minutes	_____	_____
10 minutes	_____	_____
10 minutes	_____	_____
10 minutes	_____	_____

Review Facts

I practiced:	Date	Helper
10 minutes	_____	_____
10 minutes	_____	_____
10 minutes	_____	_____
10 minutes	_____	_____
10 minutes	_____	_____
10 minutes	_____	_____

Return completed record to your teacher.

Grade 4, Just the Facts

Just the Facts

30 Minutes

CONGRATULATIONS

on your hard work practicing your _____ facts.

_____
Teacher's Signature

Practice Award

Just the Facts

60 Minutes

Practice Award

CONGRATULATIONS

on your hard work practicing your

_____ facts.

_____
Student's Name

_____
Teacher's Signature

CONGRATULATIONS

on your hard work practicing your _____ facts.

_____
Teacher's Signature

Practice Award

CONGRATULATIONS

on your hard work practicing your

_____

Student's Name

_____ facts.

_____

Teacher's Signature

Just the Facts

120 Minutes

Just the Facts
Answers

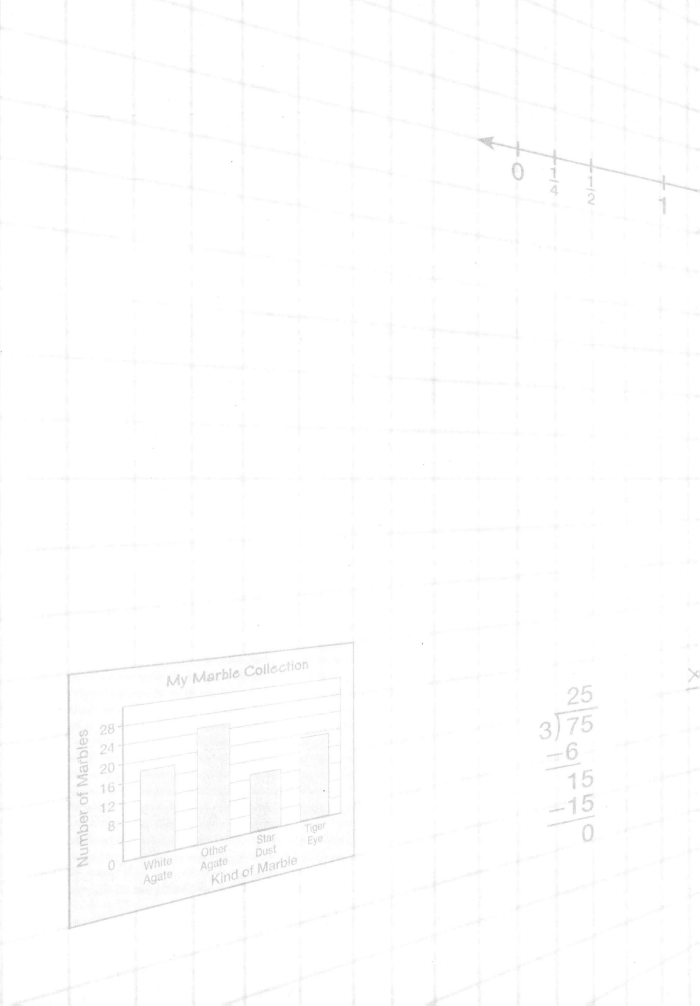

0    $\frac{1}{4}$ $\frac{1}{2}$ 1

My Marble Collection

Number of Marbles

28
24
20
16
12
8
0

White Agate   Other Agate   Star Dust   Tiger Eye

Kind of Marble

```
      25
   3)75
    -6
     15
    -15
      0
```

Level 3

Page 65

1. 6	2. 8	3. 9	4. 7	5. 9
6. 1	7. 8	8. 10	9. 8	10. 6

11. 7, 8, 9, 4 + 6 = 10   12. 6, 7, 8, 6 + 3 = 9
13. 5, 6, 7, 10 − 2 = 8   14. 4, 3, 2, 9 − 8 = 1

Page 66

1. 7	2. 7	3. 7	4. 10	5. 8	6. 9
7. 11	8. 8	9. 6	10. 2	11. 3	12. 2
13. 3	14. 4	15. 1	16. 2	17. 3	18. 2
19. 1	20. 3	21. 3	22. 3	23. 4	24. 6
25. 6	26. 6	27. 4	28. 1	29. 2	

Page 67

Answers will vary for doubles.

1. 11	2. 17	3. 13	4. 11	5. 17	6. 15
7. 2	8. 3	9. 2	10. 5	11. 4	12. 8
13. 2	14. 6	15. 4	16. 1	17. 8	18. 11
19. 14	20. 17				

Page 68

1. 8	2. 13	3. 10	4. 9	5. 9	6. 18
7. 10	8. 6	9. 11	10. 15	11. 16	12. 3
13. 12	14. 14	15. 10	16. B, 8	17. C, 4	18. A, 9

Page 69

1. 14	2. 11	3. 13	4. 14	5. 13	6. 16
7. 17	8. 12	9. 15	10. 7	11. 2	12. 2
13. 3	14. 5	15. 4	16. 8	17. 10	18. 2
19. 2	20. 3	21. 3	22. 1	23. 6	24. 2
25. 8	26. 3	27. 2	28. 6	29. 4	

Page 70

1. 5	2. 6	3. 8	4. 3	5. 6	6. 9
7. 15	8. 8	9. 13	10. 9	11. 8	12. 14
13. 5	14. 6	15. 15	16. 5	17. 12	18. 4
19. 8	20. 16	21. 5	22. 7	23. 11	24. 16
25. 9	26. 7	27. 2	28. 9	29. 8	30. 5

Page 71

1-2: Answers will vary. Possible answers are given.
1. 5 + 5 + 5 = 15, 5 × 3 = 15
2. 7 + 7 = 14, 7 × 2 = 14
3. 4, 4   4. 6, 6   5. 8, 8   6. 10, 10   7. 18   8. 16
9-11: Drawings will vary.
9. 14   10. 12   11. 8

Page 72

1-3: Drawings will vary.

1. 18	2. 24	3. 15	4. 14	5. 12	6. 18
7. 8	8. 16	9. 10	10. 6	11. 18	12. 4
13. 15	14. 12	15. 21	16. <	17. >	18. >
19. >	20. >	21. >			

Page 73

1. 2	2. 6	3. 4	4. 7	5. 12	6. 1
7. 7	8. 18	9. 8	10. 5	11. 8	12. 6
13. 4	14. 4	15. 3	16. 10	17. 14	18. 6
19. 8	20. 9	21. 10	22. 0	23. 16	24. 6
25. 8	26. 4				

Page 74

1. 6	2. 10	3. 8	4. 18	5. 4	6. 16
7. 4	8. 8	9. 12	10. 9	11. 3	12. 4
13. 5	14. 14	15. 18	16. 2	17. 7	18. 10
19. 9	20. 2	21. 1	22. 6	23. 16	24. 4
25. 12	26. 8	27. 3	28. 6	29. 14	30. 8

Page 75

1-2: Answers will vary. Possible answers are given.
1. 4 + 4 = 8, 4 × 2 = 8
2. 4 + 4 + 4 = 12, 4 × 3 = 12

3. 12	4. 32	5. 28	6. 20	7. 8	8. 16
9. 28	10. 16	11. 12	12. 36	13. 20	14. 24
15. 12	16. 28	17. 32	18. 8		

Page 76

1. 14	2. 12	3. 18	4. 8	5. 16	6. 10
7. 6	8. 18	9. 4	10. 12	11. 32	12. 28
13. 20	14. 8	15. 16	16. 36	17. 24	18. 32
19. 4	20. 8	21. 24	22. 28	23. 4	24. 36
25. 12	26. 20	27. 24	28. 32	29. 8	30. 28

Page 77

1. 6	2. 15	3. 18	4. 12	5. 27	6. 24
7. 21	8. 9	9. 27	10. 15	11. 18	12. 6
13. 12	14. 14	15. 6	16. 8	17. 10	18. 9
19. 18	20. 4	21. 8	22. 5		

Page 78

1. c	2. d	3. b	4. f
5. g	6. a	7. e	

8-17: Answers will vary. Possible answers are given.

8. 2 × 2	9. 4 × 2	10. 3 × 1	11. 1 × 5
12. 2 × 3	13. 5 × 2	14. 1 × 7	15. 3 × 3
16. 6 × 2	17. 5 × 3		

Page 79

1. 18	2. 30	3. 12	4. 24	5. 0	6. 6
7. 24	8. 54	9. 48	10. 12	11. >	12. =
13. <	14. =	15. 18	16. 0	17. 54	18. 30
19. 6	20. 42	21. 12	22. 24	23. 36	24. 48
25. 18	26. 30				

Page 80

1-2: Drawings will vary.
1. 18	**2.** 12	**3.** 36	**4.** 24	**5.** 54	**6.** 18
7. 12	**8.** 42	**9.** 48	**10.** 24	**11.** 0	**12.** 48
13. 18	**14.** 30	**15.** 24	**16.** 6	**17.** 6	

Page 81

1. 15	**2.** 30	**3.** 35	**4.** 10	**5.** 40	**6.** 20
7. 45	**8.** 30	**9.** 40	**10.** 45	**11.** >	**12.** <
13. >	**14.** >	**15.** 36	**16.** 12	**17.** 48	**18.** 42
19. 54					

Page 82

1. 10, 10   **2.** 15, 15   **3.** 20, 20
4. 40, equal to   **5.** 30, less than   **6.** 10, less than
7. 45, greater than   **8.** 50, greater than
9. 40	**10.** 15	**11.** 16	**12.** 45	**13.** 20	**14.** 30
15. 0	**16.** 35	**17.** 10			

Page 83

1. 9	**2.** 18	**3.** 27	**4.** 36	**5.** 45	**6.** 18
7. 36	**8.** 9	**9.** 4	**10.** 63	**11.** 36	**12.** 27
13. 18	**14.** 36	**15.** 72	**16.** 45	**17.** 81	**18.** 27
19. 18					

Page 84

1. 9	**2.** 18	**3.** 27	**4.** 36	**5.** 45	**6.** 54
7. 63	**8.** 72	**9.** 81	**10.** 36	**11.** 54	**12.** 20
13. 42	**14.** 63	**15.** 45	**16.** 9	**17.** 0	**18.** 9
19. 27	**20.** 1	**21.** 4	**22.** 1	**23.** 5	

Page 85

1. 21, less than   **2.** 56, greater than
3. 42, greater than   **4.** 35, greater than
5. 21	**6.** 28	**7.** 42	**8.** 35	**9.** 35
10. 56	**11.** 14	**12.** 7	**13.** 0	**14.** 63
15. >	**16.** <	**17.** <	**18.** >	

Page 86

1. 56	**2.** 21	**3.** 63	**4.** 42	**5.** 49	**6.** 49
7. 48	**8.** 7	**9.** 56	**10.** 28	**11.** 21	**12.** 28
13. 42	**14.** 63	**15.** 56	**16.** 27	**17.** 14	**18.** 59
19. 30	**20.** 18	**21.** 24			

Page 87

1. 48	**2.** 56	**3.** 24	**4.** 48	**5.** 40	**6.** 56
7. 32	**8.** 0	**9.** 64	**10.** 8	**11.** 16	**12.** 8
13. 56	**14.** 32	**15.** 5	**16.** 42	**17.** 12	**18.** 18
19. 25					

Page 88

1. 56	**2.** 40	**3.** 24
4. 8	**5.** 32	**6.** 16
7. 32	**8.** 8	**9.** 48

10. 4, 6, 10, 12, 14, 16, 18
11. 6, 9, 15, 18, 21, 24, 27
12. 8, 12, 20, 24, 28, 32, 36
13. 10, 15, 25, 30, 35, 40, 45
14. 12, 18, 30, 36, 42, 48, 54
15. 14, 21, 35, 42, 49, 56, 63
16. 16, 24, 40, 48, 56, 64, 72
17. 18, 27, 45, 54, 63, 72, 81
18. >	**19.** <	**20.** <
21. =	**22.** >	**23.** <

Level 4

Page 89

1. $3 \times 4 = 12$, $4 \times 3 = 12$
2. $3 \times 6 = 18$, $6 \times 3 = 18$
3. $3 \times 5 = 15$, $5 \times 3 = 15$
4. 5, 4   **5.** 6, 2   **6.** 3, 7   **7.** 2, 8
8. $3 \times 7 = 21$ **9.** $5 \times 5 = 25$
10. $12 \div 2 = 6$ or $12 \div 6 = 2$
11. $15 \div 3 = 5$ or $15 \div 5 = 3$

Page 90

Drawings will vary.
1. 6	**2.** 16	**3.** 18	**4.** 16	**5.** 15	**6.** 8
7. 14	**8.** 12	**9.** 10	**10.** 12	**11.** 9	**12.** 20

13-21: Drawings will vary.
13. 4	**14.** 5	**15.** 2
16. 6	**17.** 3	**18.** 9	**19.** 5	**20.** 4	**21.** 8

Page 91

1. $4 \div 2 = 2$ **2.** $10 \div 5 = 2$ **3.** $12 \div 6 = 2$
4. 2, 4, 6, 8, 10, 12, 14, 16, 18, 20
5. Drawings will vary.   **6.** Drawings will vary.
7. ÷   **8.** ×   **9.** +
10. 2, $4 \times 2 = 8$ or $2 \times 4 = 8$
11. 1, $5 \times 1 = 5$ or $1 \times 5 = 5$
12. 2, $2 \times 1 = 2$ or $1 \times 2 = 2$
13. 2, $2 \times 7 = 14$ or $7 \times 2 = 14$

Page 92

1. 14	**2.** 12	**3.** 18	**4.** 8	**5.** 16	**6.** 10
7. 6	**8.** 2	**9.** 4	**10.** 10	**11.** 6	**12.** 16
13. 18	**14.** 8	**15.** 12	**16.** 4	**17.** 3	**18.** 9
19. 5	**20.** 8	**21.** 6	**22.** 7	**23.** 2	**24.** 2

25. 14, $14 \div 7 = 2$ or $14 \div 2 = 7$
26. 6, $6 \div 3 = 2$ or $6 \div 2 = 3$
27. 8, $8 \div 4 = 2$ or $8 \div 2 = 4$
28. 16, $16 \div 8 = 2$ or $16 \div 2 = 8$

Page 93

1. 4   2. 8   3. 3
4. 7   5. 4   6. 4
7. 4   8. 4   9. 6
10. 4, 8, 12, 16, 20, 24, 28, 32, 36, 40
11. 5, 5 × 2 = 10 or 2 × 5 = 10
12. 2, 2 × 4 = 8 or 4 × 2 = 8
13. 4, 4 × 4 = 16
14. 7, 7 × 2 = 14 or 2 × 7 = 14
15. 6, 6 × 4 = 24 or 4 × 6 = 24
16. 5, 5 × 4 = 20 or 4 × 5 = 20
17. 8, 8 × 4 = 32 or 4 × 8 = 32
18. 9, 9 × 2 = 18 or 2 × 9 = 18
19. 7, 7 × 4 = 28 or 4 × 7 = 28

Page 94

1. 2, 2 × 4 = 8 or 4 × 2 = 8
2. 8, 8 × 4 = 32 or 4 × 8 = 32
3. 6, 6 × 4 = 24 or 4 × 6 = 24
4. 4, 4 × 4 = 16
5. 9, 9 × 4 = 36 or 4 × 9 = 36
6. 3, 3 × 4 = 12 or 4 × 3 = 12
7. 7, 7 × 4 = 28 or 4 × 7 = 28
8. 5, 5 × 4 = 20 or 4 × 5 = 20
9. 3, 3 × 4 = 12 or 4 × 3 = 12
10. 24   11. 20   12. 28   13. 32   14. 36
15. 12   16. 16   17. 36   18. 32   19. 20
20. 12   21. 14   22. 24

Page 95

1. 40   2. 15   3. 10   4. 25
5. 40   6. 45   7. 30   8. 30
9. 5, 10, 15, 20, 25, 30, 35, 40, 45, 50
10. 8   11. 7   12. 5   13. 2   14. 4   15. 6
16. 3   17. 9   18. 5   19. 5   20. 5   21. 5

Page 96

1. 5   2. 6   3. 9   4. 8
5. 7   6. 10   7. 3   8. 4
9. 4, 8, 12, 16, 20, 24, 28, 32, 36, 40, 44, 48
10. 9, 5   11. 5   12. 35   13. 40   14. 21
15. 9   16. 9, 6   17. 4, 5   18. 5   19. 5, 6
20. 5   21. 45   22. 3   23. 24   24. 3

Page 97

1. 8   2. 12   3. 1   4. 10   5. 2   6. 7
7. 5   8. 9   9. 2   10. 1   11. 6   12. 8
13. 4   14. 6   15. 7   16. 3
17. 1, 1 × 5 = 5 or 5 × 1 = 5
18. 3, 1 × 3 = 3 or 3 × 1 = 3
19. 5   20. 1   21. 8   22. 3

Page 98

1. 4   2. 8   3. 12   4. 9   5. 3   6. 8
7. 5   8. 7   9. 18   10. 4   11. 7   12. 20
13. 9   14. 2   15. 2   16. 6   17. 32   18. 4
19. 14   20. 4   21. 6   22. 2   23. 9   24. 12
25. 8   26. 5   27. 6   28. 8   29. 8   30. 11
31. 4

Page 99

1. 6, 3, 6, 2   2. 18, 3, 18, 6   3. 24, 8, 24, 3
4. 27, 3, 27, 9   5. 15, 5, 15, 3
6. 3 × 4 = 12, 4 × 3 = 12, 12 ÷ 3 = 4, 12 ÷ 4 = 3
7. 3 × 7 = 21, 7 × 3 = 21, 21 ÷ 3 = 7, 21 ÷ 7 = 3

Page 100

1. 2; 2, 3, 6   2. 7; 7, 3, 21   3. 4; 4, 3, 12
4. 1; 1, 3, 3   5. 3; 3, 3, 9   6. 8; 8, 3, 24
7. 5; 5, 3, 15   8. 0; 0, 3, 0   9. 6; 6, 3, 18
10. 9; 9, 3, 27
11. incorrect; corrections will vary.
12. correct; 3 × 3 = 9
13. incorrect; corrections will vary.

Page 101

1. 0   2. 8   3. 0   4. 9   5. 0   6. 0
7. 5   8. 0   9. 0   10. 7   11. 25   12. 0
13. 2   14. 0   15. 0   16. 4   17. 3   18. 12
19. 14   20. 9   21. 21   22. 24   23. 15   24. 12
25. 10   26. 20   27. 8   28. 16   29. 0

Page 102

1. 5   2. 0   3. 4   4. 0   5. 2   6. 0
7. 9   8. 1   9. 5   10. 8   11. 3   12. 0
13. 1   14. 0   15. 4   16. 7
17. 0, 0 × 4 = 0 or 4 × 0 = 0
18. 1, 1 × 5 = 5 or 5 × 1 = 5
19. 3, 3 × 1 = 3 or 1 × 3 = 3
20. 5, 5 × 2 = 10 or 2 × 5 = 10
21. 2, 2 × 3 = 6 or 3 × 2 = 6
22. 0, 0 × 3 = 0 or 3 × 0 = 0
23. 8, 8 × 1 = 8 or 1 × 8 = 8
24. 7, 7 × 2 = 14 or 2 × 7 = 14
25. 4, 4 × 1 = 4 or 1 × 4 = 4
26. 3, 3 × 3 = 9
27. 1, 1 × 3 = 3 or 3 × 1 = 3
28. 16, 16 × 1 = 16 or 1 × 16 = 16

Page 103

1. 9 × 3 = 27, 3 × 9 = 27
2. 9 × 2 = 18, 2 × 9 = 18
3. 9   4. 8   5. 6
6. 6, 6 or 9, 4   7. 2, 9 or 3, 6   8. 9, 5
9. 45   10. 63   11. 27   12. 36   13. 81
14. 54   15. 45   16. 18   17. 9   18. 72

Page 104

1. 0	**2.** 9	**3.** 5	**4.** 1	**5.** 9	**6.** 3
7. 3	**8.** 2	**9.** 5	**10.** 7	**11.** 4	**12.** 9
13. 8	**14.** 3	**15.** 6	**16.** >	**17.** =	**18.** <
19. <	**20.** 9	**21.** 9	**22.** 3	**23.** 1	**24.** 4
25. 9	**26.** 9	**27.** 9			

Page 105

1. 9, 18	**2.** 6, 12	**3.** 21, 42	**4.** 12, 24	
5. 27, 54	**6.** 15, 30	**7.** 24, 48	**8.** 18, 36	
9. 24	**10.** 18	**11.** 30	**12.** 42	**13.** 36
14. 6	**15.** 12	**16.** 0	**17.** 54	**18.** 48
19. 30	**20.** 42	**21.** 24	**22.** 18	**23.** 21
24. 12	**25.** 48	**26.** 54	**27.** 25	**28.** 16

Page 106

1. 6, 7, 42; 7, 6, 42; 42, 7, 6; 42, 6, 7
2. 5, 6, 30; 6, 5, 30; 30, 6, 5; 30, 5, 6
3. 6, 8, 48; 8, 6, 48; 48, 8, 6; 48, 6, 8
4. 6, 9, 54; 9, 6, 54; 54, 9, 6; 54, 6, 9
5. 6, 4, 24; 4, 6, 24; 24, 4, 6; 24, 6, 4

Page 107

1. 1; 1, 7, 7   **2.** 3; 3, 7, 21   **3.** 5; 5, 7, 35
4. 8; 8, 7, 56   **5.** 6; 6, 7, 42   **6.** 9; 9, 7, 63
7. 2; 2, 7, 14   **8.** 4; 4, 7, 28   **9.** 7; 7, 7, 49
10. 7, 9, 63; 9, 7, 63; 63, 9, 7; 63, 7, 9
11. 7, 8, 56; 8, 7, 56; 56, 8, 7; 56, 7, 8

Page 108

1. 14	**2.** 35	**3.** 49	**4.** 28	**5.** 21	**6.** 56
7. 63	**8.** 42	**9.** 7	**10.** 0	**11.** 14	**12.** 42
13. 56	**14.** 28	**15.** 7	**16.** 63	**17.** 35	**18.** 49
19. 21	**20.** 0	**21.** 7	**22.** 9	**23.** 3	**24.** 1
25. 2	**26.** 8	**27.** 6	**28.** 4	**29.** 7	**30.** 5

Page 109

1. $3 \times 8 = 24$, $8 \times 3 = 24$
2. $2 \times 8 = 16$, $8 \times 2 = 16$
3. $4 \times 8 = 32$, $8 \times 4 = 32$
4. $6 \times 8 = 48$ **5.** $5 \times 8 = 40$ **6.** $7 \times 8 = 56$
7. $9 \times 8 = 72$ **8.** $4 \times 8 = 32$ **9.** $8 \times 8 = 64$
10. Drawings will vary, 48 **11.** Drawings will vary, 24
12. 48   **13.** 40   **14.** 56   **15.** 32

Page 110

1. 5	**2.** 7	**3.** 3	**4.** 8	**5.** 6
6. 9	**7.** 8, 9	**8.** 7, 8	**9.** 3, 8	**10.** 4
11. 2	**12.** 5	**13.** 3	**14.** 6	**15.** 1
16. 7	**17.** 8			

18-23: incorrect; corrections will vary.

Page 111

1. 32	**2.** 18	**3.** 40	**4.** 36	**5.** 64	**6.** 27
7. 63	**8.** 8	**9.** 45	**10.** 63	**11.** 81	**12.** 48
13. 72	**14.** 27	**15.** 56	**16.** 48	**17.** 45	**18.** 16
19. 49	**20.** 40	**21.** 56	**22.** 24	**23.** 36	**24.** 28
25. 54	**26.** 42	**27.** 27	**28.** 24	**29.** 36	**30.** 14

Page 112

1. 4	**2.** 5	**3.** 1	**4.** 8	**5.** 4
6. 9	**7.** 6	**8.** 1	**9.** 7	**10.** 8
11. 3	**12.** 9	**13.** 5	**14.** 0	**15.** 2
16. 0	**17.** 6	**18.** 0	**19.** 7	**20.** 9
21. 6	**22.** 8	**23.** 5	**24.** 1	**25.** 4
26. 2	**27.** 2	**28.** 6	**29.** 4	**30.** 9
31. 3	**32.** 8	**33.** 6	**34.** 7	**35.** 3

Page 113

1. 7, 4, 28; 4, 7, 28; 28, 4, 7; 28, 7, 4
2. 8, 3, 24; 3, 8, 24; 24, 3, 8; 24, 8, 3
3. 21, 63, 42, 49
4. 27, 7, 6, 5, 81
5. 27   **6.** 36   **7.** 72   **8.** 45   **9.** 81

Page 114

1. $5 \times 7 = 35$; $7 \times 5 = 35$; $35 \div 7 = 5$; $35 \div 5 = 7$
2. $6 \times 8 = 48$; $8 \times 6 = 48$; $48 \div 8 = 6$; $48 \div 6 = 8$
3. 32, 4, 32, 8   **4.** 42, 6, 42, 7
5. 40, 8, 40, 5   **6.** 36, 4, 36, 9
7. 5   **8.** 8   **9.** 9   **10.** 4

Cumulative Practice

Page 115

1. 9	**2.** 6	**3.** 7	**4.** 7	**5.** 10	**6.** 5
7. 9	**8.** 17	**9.** 11	**10.** 11	**11.** 15	**12.** 8
13. 18	**14.** 1	**15.** 8	**16.** 10	**17.** 14	**18.** 13
19. 10	**20.** 12	**21.** 6	**22.** 6	**23.** 16	**24.** 8
25. 12	**26.** 10	**27.** 12	**28.** 13	**29.** 12	**30.** 10

Page 116

1. 4	**2.** 15	**3.** 10	**4.** 9	**5.** 9	**6.** 9
7. 5	**8.** 3	**9.** 17	**10.** 13	**11.** 11	**12.** 13
13. 5	**14.** 13	**15.** 11	**16.** 11	**17.** 4	**18.** 16
19. 7	**20.** 4	**21.** 15	**22.** 12	**23.** 11	**24.** 7
25. 2	**26.** 14	**27.** 7	**28.** 6	**29.** 5	**30.** 0

Page 117

1. 7	**2.** 7	**3.** 17	**4.** 7	**5.** 2	**6.** 9
7. 3	**8.** 9	**9.** 10	**10.** 13	**11.** 8	**12.** 4
13. 12	**14.** 5	**15.** 11	**16.** 6	**17.** 15	**18.** 5
19. 12	**20.** 10	**21.** 11	**22.** 1	**23.** 10	**24.** 3
25. 6	**26.** 14	**27.** 14	**28.** 4	**29.** 16	**30.** 9

Page 118

1. 6	2. 8	3. 2	4. 1	5. 7	6. 5
7. 3	8. 4	9. 3	10. 9	11. 3	12. 0
13. 6	14. 0	15. 5	16. 0	17. 9	18. 4
19. 9	20. 7	21. 9	22. 7	23. 5	24. 1
25. 1	26. 1	27. 9	28. 4	29. 4	30. 7

Page 119

1. 4	2. 0	3. 9	4. 8	5. 8	6. 6
7. 2	8. 1	9. 6	10. 1	11. 2	12. 0
13. 5	14. 8	15. 8	16. 9	17. 4	18. 9
19. 2	20. 7	21. 7	22. 8	23. 4	24. 1
25. 0	26. 2	27. 5	28. 2	29. 6	30. 9

Page 120

1. 7	2. 1	3. 5	4. 8	5. 0	6. 4
7. 5	8. 8	9. 9	10. 0	11. 6	12. 4
13. 5	14. 6	15. 3	16. 1	17. 8	18. 3
19. 3	20. 3	21. 1	22. 7	23. 7	24. 6
25. 5	26. 9	27. 2	28. 2	29. 6	30. 1

Page 121

1. 10	2. 4	3. 56	4. 0	5. 12	6. 18
7. 54	8. 36	9. 0	10. 14	11. 48	12. 30
13. 35	14. 15	15. 28	16. 18	17. 16	18. 9
19. 12	20. 0	21. 63	22. 35	23. 12	24. 42
25. 21	26. 24	27. 40	28. 32	29. 9	30. 45

Page 122

1. 0	2. 63	3. 25	4. 18	5. 2	6. 24
7. 12	8. 0	9. 7	10. 6	11. 64	12. 45
13. 18	14. 27	15. 9	16. 6	17. 0	18. 4
19. 49	20. 20	21. 5	22. 21	23. 54	24. 0
25. 18	26. 3	27. 42	28. 72	29. 12	30. 36

Page 123

1. 1	2. 56	3. 20	4. 18	5. 0	6. 8
7. 72	8. 8	9. 6	10. 10	11. 28	12. 0
13. 30	14. 21	15. 48	16. 12	17. 40	18. 32
19. 81	20. 0	21. 16	22. 0	23. 24	24. 12
25. 4	26. 15	27. 0	28. 27	29. 54	30. 36

Page 124

1. 6	2. 4	3. 3	4. 9	5. 0	6. 6
7. 9	8. 5	9. 1	10. 7	11. 7	12. 2
13. 5	14. 8	15. 1	16. 9	17. 3	18. 3
19. 7	20. 3	21. 9	22. 2	23. 0	24. 6
25. 3	26. 6	27. 7	28. 4	29. 5	30. 9

Page 125

1. 7	2. 8	3. 0	4. 2	5. 5	6. 8
7. 1	8. 3	9. 7	10. 2	11. 5	12. 5
13. 8	14. 6	15. 0	16. 4	17. 2	18. 3
19. 6	20. 1	21. 9	22. 8	23. 5	24. 2
25. 4	26. 0	27. 8	28. 7	29. 1	30. 5

Page 126

1. 4	2. 6	3. 3	4. 1	5. 6	6. 4
7. 5	8. 2	9. 0	10. 8	11. 0	12. 8
13. 7	14. 9	15. 8	16. 1	17. 6	18. 3
19. 9	20. 0	21. 9	22. 1	23. 4	24. 0
25. 9	26. 4	27. 2	28. 4	29. 7	30. 1